A SHORT INTRODUCTION TO MODERN GROWTH THEORY

Ching-yao Hsieh
Ahmad A. Abushaikha
Anne Richards
The George Washington University

University Press of America

Copyright © 1978 by

University Press of America, Inc.™

4710 Auth Place, S.E., Washington, D.C. 20023

ISBN: 0-8191-0628-3

Library of Congress Catalog Card Number: 78-61916

To two wives and a mother:

Linda, Fatima, and Ruth

PREFACE

This book is a simplified, concise yet comprehensive introduction to economic growth theory. It is designed to be used as a textbook for a specialized graduate course on growth theory and as a companion for any textbook used in intermediate and graduate macroeconomics courses.

We realize that growth theory is wide in scope and complicated in technique and that it is impossible to cover all its aspects in such a short introduction. We had to face the formidable task of making the subject as simple and manageable as possible. But at the same time, we were careful to cover the bulk of the different theories and controversies and to provide the relevant references to those readers who wish to pursue detailed study of certain aspects of growth theory.

The modern library is full of excellent references on growth theory. The bulk of them, however, are so full of details that the readers are sometimes left wandering where they are. In this text we tried to avoid this complication by attempting to give as comprehensive a picture as possible, and to provide only the details we sensed were relevant and necessary to highlight the idea under discussion.

Growth theories are much older than that of Harrod's, yet we have chosen to take Harrod's as our point of departure because it represents a new era of formal investigation of the functioning of the economic system over time; we then proceed to the Neoclassical and the Post-Keynesian paradigms. In the

last chapter of this book, we provide a tentative
evaluation of the alternative theories of growth
in an attempt not to settle issues but to create
the incentive for the reader to further investigate this worthwhile aspect of economic theory.

George Washington University   C. Y. Hsieh
                                      A. Abushaikha
                                      A. Richards

TABLE OF CONTENTS

CHAPTER 1

INTRODUCTION

Ever since the publication of Professor
Solow's seminal paper, "A Contribution to the Theory
of Economic Growth" (1956), the majority of growth
models have been formulated in the neoclassical paradigm. The background of the neoclassical paradigm is
the "neoclassical synthesis," the essence of which is
stated by Professor Samuelson as follows:

> By means of appropriately reinforcing monetary
> and fiscal policies, our mixed enterprise system
> can avoid the excess of boom and slump and can
> look forward to healthy progressive growth. This
> fundamental being understood, the paradoxes that
> robbed the older classical principles dealing with
> small-scale "microeconomics" of much of their
> relevance and validity will now lose their sting.
> In short, mastery of the modern analysis of in-
> come determination genuinely validates the basic
> classical principles; and the economist is now
> justified in saying that the broad cleavage be-
> tween microeconomics and macroeconomics has been
> closed. 1/

The formative years of the synthesis span from 1937
to 1956. They started with the formulation of Hicksian IS-LM analysis and peaked with the integration of
monetary and value theory so carefully stated by Professor Patinkin. 2/ The framework of the in-theory

---

1/ Paul A. Samuelson, ECONOMICS, 6th edition (New
York: McGraw-Hill, 1964), pp. 360-361.

2/ J. R. Hicks, "Mr. Keynes and the 'Classics': A
Suggested Interpretation," ECONOMETRICA, April

1

belief is Walrasian general equilibrium analysis and
the indispensable tool of this analysis is the "real
balance" effect. The general conclusions of the synthesis imply that Keynesian involuntary unemployment
with its corollary of unneutrality of money may be
regarded as special cases of the "neoclassical" general equilibrium models, for they depend upon certain
special assumptions such as price rigidities, or the
presence of one of the following factors: money illu-
sion, distribution effects, or nonunitary elasticity
of price expectations. 3/ Although Keynes's theoretical contributions have been significantly downgraded
by the new interpretations, the in-theory belief permits the coexistence of Keynesian full-employment
policy. Professor Patinkin writes:

> But this narrowing of the analytical distance
> between Keynesian and classical economics does
> not generate a corresponding narrowing of the
> policy distance. It still leaves Keynes insist-
> ing that the inefficacy of the automatic adjust-
> ing process is so great as to be remediable only
> by a program of direct government investment in
> public works. 4/

The microfoundation of the neoclassical growth
models is the marginal theory of value and distribution. Yet, "placing reliance upon neoclassical economic theory is a matter of faith." 5/ This faith is

---

1937; Don Patinkin, MONEY, INTEREST, AND PRICES,
1st edition (Evanston, Ill.: Harper & Row, 1956).

3/ See Don Patinkin, op. cit., 2nd ed., 1965,
Chapter XIV.

4/ Don Patinkin, op. cit., 2nd ed., 1965, p. 340.

5/ C. E. Ferguson, THE NEOCLASSICAL THEORY OF PRODUC-
TION AND DISTRIBUTION (Great Britain: Cambridge
University Press, 1969), p. xvii.

aptly expressed by Professor Samuelson:

> Until the laws of thermodynamics are repealed, I shall continue to relate outputs to inputs--i.e. to believe in production functions. Until factors cease to have their rewards determined by bidding in quasi-competitive markets, I shall adhere to (generalized) neoclassical approximations in which relative factor supplies are important in explaining their market remunerations. . . . a many-sectored neoclassical model with heterogeneous capital goods and somewhat limited factor substitutions can fail to have some of the simple properties of the idealized J. B. Clark neoclassical models. Recognizing these complications does not justify nihilism or refuge in theories that neglect short-term microeconomic pricing. 6/

The relevance of the marginal theory of value and distribution has been questioned by a number of writers on both sides of the Atlantic. The American tradition focuses on the irrelevance of Walras's law and its special assumption of the tâtonnement process. The spokesmen are Robert Clower and Axel Leijonhufvud. 7/ They assert that once the tâtonnement process and the deus ex machina, the auctioneer, are removed from general equilibrium analysis, a disequilibrium state will prevail. The manifestations of the disequilibrium state are: imperfect and costly information, reservation prices, false trading, quantity adjustments,

---

6/ Paul A. Samuelson. See the flyleaf quotation of Ferguson's book, op. cit.

7/ Robert W. Clower, "The Keynesian Counter-Revolution: A Theoretical Appraisal," in THE THEORY OF INTEREST RATES, edited by F. H. Hahn and F. Brechling (London: Macmillan, 1965), Chapter 5, reprinted in MONETARY THEORY, edited by R. W. Clower, Penguin Modern Economics Readings, 1969, pp. 270-297; Axel Leijonhufvud, ON KEYNESIAN ECONOMICS AND THE ECONOMICS OF KEYNES (London: Oxford University Press, 1968).

3

search unemployment, and the "dual-decision (two-stage)" process.8/ Thus, even in a world of rational decision-maki by transactors, Keynesian unemployment can exist.9/ Hence, Professor Clower observes: "Keynesian economics is price theory without Walras' law, and price theory with Walras' law is just a special case of Keynesian economics."10/

One the other side of the Atlantic, the economists of Cambridge, England, argue that value and distribution theories are not two sides of the same coin.11/ In the tradition of Ricardo and Marx, they insist that distributioɪ should precede value in priority and should not be derived from within the circle of exchange. Since Neoclassical theory "is a beautiful edifice erected upon the foundation of" the linearly homogenous aggregate production function,1: the marginal productivity theory of distribution will crumb once the aggregateproduction function is discredited; and to destroy the aggregate production function it is

---

8/ See R. W. Clower, op. cit., pp. 287-290, for the explanation of the "dual-decision hypothesis."

9/ See R. W. Clower and Leijonhufvud, op. cit.

10/ R. W. Clower, op. cit., p. 295.

11/ The writers of this School have been called by various names, such as "Neo-Keynesians," "Anglo-Italian Scjool," "Neo-Ricardians," and "post-Keynesians." The advocates of the new approach include: Joan Robinson, Kaldor, Kregel, Pasinetti, Nuti, Sraffa, and others in England; Garegnani and Spaventa in Italy; Asimakopoulos and Harcourt in Australia; Bhaduri and Bharadwaj in India; Rymes in Canada; and Nell, Davidson, Weintraub, Clower, and Leijonhufvud in U.S.A.

12/ C. E. Ferguson, op. cit., pp. 11-12.

necessary to question the validity of the Clarkian homogeneous real capital contained therein. Thus, the first salvo was fired by Professor Joan Robinson concerning the search for a unit of measurement of the aggregate social capital.13/ This was the beginning of the controversy over capital reversal and double-switching. The long, drawn out debate has been lucidly documented by Professor G. C. Harcourt in his scholarly book, SOME CAMBRIDGE CONTROVERSIES IN THE THEORY OF CAPITAL (1972).14/

The alternative paradigm in growth theory, however, is not tied only to the arguments about capital reversal and double-switching. Alfred S. Eichner and J. A. Kregel recently observed:

> Trying to grasp the potential (of the post-Keynesian paradigm in economic theory) from the arguments about capital reversal and double-switching, however, is likely to be just as treacherous as trying to understand the marginal revolution of the late 19th century from the debate over the "wages fund" doctrine.15/

The crucial difference between the neoclassical and post-Keynesian paradigms in growth theory is

---

13/ Joan Robinson, "The Production Function and the Theory of Capital," in her COLLECTED PAPERS, Vol. 2 (Oxford: Blackwell, 1960). The paper was first published in REVIEW OF ECONOMIC STUDIES, Vol. 21 (1953-4), pp. 81-106.

14/ G. C. Harcourt, SOME CAMBRIDGE CONTROVERSIES IN THE THEORY OF CAPITAL (England: Cambridge University Press, 1972).

15/ Alfred S. Eichner and J. A. Kregel, "An Essay on Post-Keynesian Theory: A New Paradigm in Economics," in JOURNAL OF ECONOMIC LITERATURE, Vol. 13, No. 4, Dec. 1975.

the assumption about investment. In the neoclassical
world, savings determine investment. Hence, the investment function is absent in practically all neoclassical growth models. This particular assumption
not only removes the Harrodian "knife-edge" problem
but also assures full-employment equilibrium growth.
For investment is the link between the past and the
future in historical time. Investment decisions are
being made in the present on the basis of expectations
about the future. Thus, Professor Joan Robinson in-
sists that it is through investment decisions that the
influences of history and of expectations are felt.
The future is uncertain. Hence, the very essence of
Keynes's problem ̤ uncertainty.16/

In the alternative paradigm, it is investment
that determines savings and not the other way around.
Furthermore, investment is being assigned to play the
key role at the micro, as well as at the macro level.
At the microeconomic level, advocates of the new approach suggest what we call a macrofoundation of the
microeconomic pricing mechanism. The direction of
causality may be shown (at the risk of being overly
simplified) as follows: (a) Historical and institutional forces shape macroeconomic conditions, (b) macroeconomic phenomena, in turn, influence investment
decisions of individual entrepreneurs, and (c) the
entrepreneurs then select the mark-up prices and
decide upon capacity utilization compatible with
investment plans.

16/ See Joan Robinson, "The Second Crisis of Economic
    Theory," Richard T. Ely Lecture, AMERICAN ECONOMIC
    REVIEW, Papers and Proceedings, December 27-29,
    1971.

At the macroeconomic level, the explicit role of investment may be seen in the "widow's cruse" theory of distribution. The direction of causality here proceeds from the effect of investment on the rate of profit which, in turn, determines the distribution of income; and distribution then affects long-run economic growth.

This book is designed to give a short introduction to the two alternative approaches to growth theory. The point of departure for both approaches is Harrod's model, which is succinctly reviewed together with Domar's model in Chapter 2. Following the brief discussion of the Harrod-Domar analysis, this book is divided into two parts. Part I deals with the prevailing neoclassical paradigm in growth theory. It consists of seven chapters. The first of these, Chapter 3, gives a brief survey of the theoretical heritage of the neoclassical paradigm, while Solow's basic neoclassical model without technical progress is covered in Chapter 4. The basic neoclassical model--first with disembodied and then with embodied technical progress--is discussed in Chapters 5 and 6, respectively. The following Chapter 7 introduces the role of money in the basic neoclassical model. The discussion in this chapter follows the seminal paper of Levhari and Patinkin.17/ It should be noted that the preceding four chapters in Part I deal with one-sector neoclassical growth models only. The simplifying assumption of the one-sector model is that there is only one production sector, which

_____

17/ D. Levhari and D. Patinkin, "The Role of Money in a Simple Growth Model," AMERICAN ECONOMIC REVIEW, Vol. LXVIII, September 1968, pp. 713-53.

produces one homogeneous output that can be transformed without cost into either a consumption good or
a capital good. Professor J. E. Meade calls this the
assumption of perfect substitutability in production
between capital and consumption goods.18/ This simplifying assumption is removed, however, in the discussion of a two-sector neoclassical growth model
contained in Chapter 8. This chapter also includes a
two-sector model of the type developed by Professors
Meade and Uzawa 19/ and a diagrammatic illustration
of it suggested by Professor Harry G. Johnson.20/
Part I closes with Chapter 9. The subject matter of
Chapter 9 is the optimal neoclassical growth model
wherein the well-known Pontryagin maximum principle is
invoked to explain the "golden rule of accumulation."

The post-Keynesian paradigm in growth theory
is introduced in Part II, which consists of five chapters. The theoretical heritage of the new paradigm is
briefly surveyed in Chapter 10. Then the reswitching
controversy in the theory of capital is outlined in
Chapter 11. The following Chapter 12 attempts to
highlight the crucial role assigned to investment in
the discussions of distribution and growth by Joan
Robinson, Kaldor, and Pasinetti. Chapter 13 contains

18/ J. E. Meade, A NEOCLASSICAL THEORY OF ECONOMIC
GROWTH (London: Allen & Unwin, 1961), p. 6.

19/ J. E. Meade, op. cit., Appendix II; and H. Uzawa,
"On a Two-Sector Model of Economic Growth, I,"
REVIEW OF ECONOMIC STATISTICS, Vol. XXIX, October
1961, pp. 40-47; and "On a Two-Sector Model of
Economic Growth, II," Vol. XXX, June 1963,
pp. 105-18.

20/ Harry G. Johnson, THE THEORY OF INCOME DISTRIBU-
TION (London: Gray-Mills, 1973), Chapter 5.

a contrast between the nonvintage and vintage models of Kaldor. Finally, the concluding Chapter 14 gives a tentative evaluation of the two alternative approaches to modern growth theory.

References

Clower, Robert W., "The Keynesian Counter-Revolution: A Theoretical Appraisal," in THE THEORY OF INTEREST RATES, edited by F. H. Hahn and F. Brechling (London: Macmillan, 1965), Chapter 5, reprinted in MONETARY THEORY, edited by R. W. Clower (Penguin Modern Economics Readings, 1969).

Eichner, A. S., and J. A. Kregel, "An Essay on Post-Keynesian Theory: A New Paradigm in Economics," Journal of Economic Literature, Vol. 13, No. 4, Dec. 1975.

Ferguson, C. E., THE NEOCLASSICAL THEORY OF PRODUCTION AND DISTRIBUTION (Great Britain: Cambridge University Press, 1969).

Harcourt, G. C., SOME CAMBRIDGE CONTROVERSIES IN THE THEORY OF CAPITAL (England: Cambridge University Press, 1972).

Hicks, J. R., "Mr. Keynes and the 'Classics': A Suggested Interpretation," Econometrica, April 1937.

Johnson, Harry G., THE THEORY OF INCOME DISTRIBUTION (London: Gray-Mills, 1973).

Leijonhufvud, Axel, ON KEYNESIAN ECONOMICS AND THE ECONOMICS OF KEYNES (London: Oxford University Press, 1968).

Levhari, D., and D. Patinkin, "The Role of Money in a Simple Growth Model," American Economic Review, Vol. LXVIII, Sept. 1968, pp. 713-53.

Meade, J. E., A NEOCLASSICAL THEORY OF ECONOMIC GROWTH (London: Allen & Unwin, 1961).

Patinkin, D., MONEY, INTEREST, AND PRICES, 1st edition (Evanston, Ill.: Harper & Row, 1956).

Robinson, Joan, COLLECTED ECONOMIC PAPERS, Vol. 2 (Oxford: Basil Blackwell, 1960).

Samuelson, Paul A., ECONOMICS, 6th edition (New York: McGraw-Hill, 1964).

Uzawa, H., "On a Two-Sector Model of Economic Growth, I," Review of Economic Studies, Vol. XXIX, Oct. 1961, pp. 40-47.

_____, "On a Two-Sector Model of Economic Growth, II" Review of Economic Studies, Vol. XXX, June 1963, pp. 105-18.

CHAPTER 2

THE POINT OF DEPARTURE OF MODERN GROWTH

THEORY -- HARROD'S MODEL

True to the Keynesian spirit, Harrod questions
the neoclassical propositions that all savings will be
automatically absorbed by investment and that price
flexibility will always assure full-employment equilibrium. Like Keynes, Harrod emphasizes the inflexi-
bility of factor prices. Thus, even if production
functions permitted factor substitutability, entrepreneurs would have no incentive to make such substi-
tutions. It should be noted that this is Harrod's
intention behind his constant capital-output ratio
assumption. To interpret it as purely a technical
coefficient would be a distortion of the Harrodian
analysis.

In order to understand Harrod's warranted rate
of growth of output, it is necessary to treat the
capital-output ratio as a behavioral coefficient expressing the entrepreneur's desired or required capital stock given the growth of output. Let us write
the constant capital-output ratio as $K/Y = \beta$, where
β stands for the behavioral coefficient. Then the
marginal capital-output ratio may be written as
$\frac{dK}{dt} \Big/ \frac{dY}{dt} = \beta$. If we transform this equation into the
form $I = \beta \frac{dY}{dt}$, the acceleration principle of investment is obtained. With this basic understanding in
mind, Harrod's model may be described as follows:

11

The three assumptions of the model are:
(a) a constant capital-output ratio, which implies
also a constant labor-output ratio, $\frac{L}{Y} = \alpha$; (b) the
level of ex ante aggregate savings is a constant
proportion of aggregate real income, or $S = sY$; and
(c) the labor force grows at a constant rate, n,
which is determined exogenously. This assumption
may be written as $L = L_o e^{nt}$.

Harrod's warranted growth rate of output
is derived from the following three simultaneous
equations:

$\quad$ (1) $\quad S = sY$

$\quad$ (2) $\quad I = \beta \frac{dY}{dt}$

$\quad$ (3) $\quad I = S.$

By substituting equations (1) and (2) into
equation (3), we have:

$\quad$ (4) $\quad \beta \frac{dY}{dt} = sY$

Dividing both sides of equation (4) by Y
and β, one finds that

$\quad$ (5) $\quad \frac{1}{Y} \frac{dY}{dt} = \frac{s}{\beta}$

Equation (5) gives the "warranted" rate of
growth of output. It is called the "warranted" rate
because it will leave entrepreneurs satisfied with the
outcome of economic activity. In other words, it is
a rate of growth of output which will induce just the
right amount of investment (via the acceleration principle) to absorb the savings generated in the current
income period (via the assumption that $S = sY$).

Equation (5) is a marginal function. [1] To

_____

[1] Equation (5) could also be solved as a first order

find the total function, namely, in the present case, the time path for Y, one integrates both sides of equation (5) with respect to time t. In doing so, one obtains the following expression:

$$(6) \quad \int \frac{1}{Y} \frac{dY}{dt} \, dt = \int \frac{s}{\beta} \, dt$$

Integrating the left side of equation (6) yields:

$$(7) \quad \int \frac{1}{Y} \frac{dY}{dt} \, dt = \log_e Y + C_1$$

where C_1 is an arbitrary constant. Integrating the right side of equation (6) yields:

$$(8) \quad \int \frac{s}{\beta} \, dt = \frac{s}{\beta} t + C_2$$

where C_2 is also an arbitrary constant. By equating the two results and combining the two constants (which will disappear in the process of differentiating the total function with respect to time), one obtains:

$$(9) \quad \log_e Y = \frac{s}{\beta} t + C \, , \quad \text{where } C = C_1 + C_2.$$

Equation (9) may be transformed into an exponential expression as follows:

$$(10) \quad Y = e^{\frac{s}{\beta} t + C} = e^{\frac{s}{\beta} t} \cdot e^C$$

Let $e^C = Y_o$. Then the time path for Y (the total function) is derived as follows:

$$(11) \quad Y = Y_o e^{\frac{s}{\beta} t}$$

If we differentiate this total function with

---

linear homogeneous differential equation. Multiply both sides of the equation by Y and then subtract $\frac{s}{\beta} Y$ from each side to get $\frac{dY}{dt} - \frac{s}{\beta} Y = 0$ The general solution to this equation is $Y = Ae^{\frac{s}{\beta} t}$ where A is a constant. The definite solution is $Y = Y_o e^{\frac{s}{\beta} t}$

respect to time, we will obtain the marginal function, namely equation (5). For indefinite integration is simply the reverse process of differentiation.

Like Keynes, Harrod thinks that the capitalist system is inherently unstable. The warranted growth rate of output and the actual growth rate of output cannot coincide all the time. Departures from the warranted rate of growth not only cannot be self-equilibrating but also would produce even larger divergences. This is Harrod's view on the short-run instability of the economic system. It has been called the "knife-edge" problem of Harrod.

The long-run prospect of steady-state growth of the economic system appears to Harrod as equally pessimistic. Thus, he introduces the concept of the natural rate of growth of output to illustrate the long-run instability problem. The natural growth rate is the ceiling or maximum rate of growth of output permitted by the growth of the labor force and labor-augmenting technical progress. 2/ The "knife-edge" problem again appears in the case of divergence between the natural rate and the warranted rate of growth of output. If the warranted rate of growth exceeds the natural rate, a collision course is the inevitable result; and if, instead, the warranted rate

---

2/ Labor-augmenting technical progress is equivalent to a corresponding increase in the labor force. Since we are considering technical progress in the context of steady-state or equilibrium growth at some constant proportional rate, it is customary to assume that technical progress also proceeds at some given proportional rate, say, m. For a more detailed discussion of Harrod's neutral labor-augmenting technical progress, see Chapter 5, Part I of this volume.

is less than the natural rate, long-run stagnation occurs. Thus, full-employment equilibrium growth requires that all three rates coincide. Let Gw stand for the warranted rate of growth of output, Ga the actual growth rate of output, and Gn the natural growth rate of output. Full-employment equilibrium growth requires: Gw = Ga = Gn, or,

$$(12) \quad \frac{1}{Y} \frac{dY}{dt} = \frac{1}{K} \frac{dK}{dt} = \frac{1}{L} \frac{dL}{dt} = \frac{s}{\beta} = n + m$$

where m stands for the rate of labor-augmenting technical progress. If Harrod's labor-augmenting technical progress is abstracted, equation (12) may be written as:

$$(13) \quad \frac{s}{\beta} = n$$

The equality expressed by either of the preceding two equations has been called the "golden age" growth rate of output. 3/

The "knife-edge" problem of Harrod is the point of departure of the adversary paradigms in modern growth theory. On one side, the neoclassical paradigm stems from Professor Solow's seminal paper of 1956. Professor Solow observes:

> . . . this fundamental opposition of warranted and natural rates turns out in the end to flow from the crucial assumption that production takes place under conditions of fixed proportions. There is no possibility of substituting labor for capital in production. If this assumption

---

3/ The term was coined by Professor Joan Robinson. See her THE ACCUMULATION OF CAPITAL (New York: St. Martin's Press, 1965), pp. 99-100. Professor Robinson remarks: "We may describe these conditions as a golden age thus indicating that it represents a mythical state of affairs not likely to obtain in any actual economy." Op. cit., p. 99.

is abandoned, the knife-edge notion of unstable balance seems to go with it. Indeed it is hardly surprising that such a gross rigidity in one part of the system should entail lack of flexibility in another.

A remarkable characteristic of the Harrod-Domar model is that it consistently studies long-run problems with the usual short-run tools. One usually thinks of the long run as the domain of neoclassical analysis, the land of the margin. Instead Harrod and Domar talk of the long run in terms of the multiplier, the accelerator, "the" capital coefficient. The bulk of this paper is devoted to a model of long-run growth which accepts all the Harrod-Domar assumptions except that of the fixed proportions. 4/

Thus the linearly homogeneous production function becomes the standard property of neoclassical growth models. Since neoclassical theory is a beautiful edifice built on the foundation of the linearly homogeneous production function, the alternative cost of removal of the "knife-edge" problem is the resurrection of the neoclassical marginal theory of value and distribution.

On the other side, the advocates of the post-Keynesian paradigm in economic theory criticize Harrod for his neglect of the determination of the rate of profit in his model. A representative criticism is voiced by Professor J. A. Kregel:

> Harrod's view of entrepreneurial behavior does, however, lead to a basic omission in the system. Harrod never considers the rate of profit. . . .

4/ Robert M. Solow, "A Contribution to the Theory of Economic Growth," QUARTERLY JOURNAL OF ECONOMICS, Vol. 70, Feb. 1956, pp. 65-94, reprinted in MACROECONOMIC THEORY: SELECTED READINGS, edited by H. R. Williams and J. D. Huffnagle (New York: Appleton-Century-Crofts, 1969), p. 425.

Harrod's neglect of the profit rate prevents him from presenting a theory of distribution which ultimately leads him first into the knife-edge and then into a basic indeterminacy. These short-comings provide the major objections to Harrod's approach. 5/

It is in the hands of Professor Kaldor and subsequently Professor Pasinetti and other writers of the "Anglo-Italian School" to put the "widow's cruse" theory of distribution into juxtaposition with long-run economic growth. Thus, the prototype of post-Keynesian growth theory was born.

Although business cycle theories are not within our purview, it should nonetheless be noted that the Harrodian "knife-edge" problem in the short run had prompted Professor Hicks to formulate his famous model of trade cycles. 6/ The Harrodian in-stability is attributed to the mathematical formula-tion of his system. Neither his saving function nor his investment function contains lagged relations. Professor Hicks writes:

> But mathematical instability does not in itself elucidate fluctuation. A mathematically unstable system does not fluctuate; it just breaks down. . . . The lags are needed to hold the system to a given path. Mr. Harrod's theory, in the form he has given it, may be regarded as an indirect proof of this; because he will have no lags, his system explodes out of time dimension. A dynamic system which is economically unstable, having a

---

5/ J. A. Kregel, RATE OF PROFIT, DISTRIBUTION AND GROWTH: TWO VIEWS (Chicago and New York: Aldine-Atherton, 1971), pp. 115-24.

6/ J. R. Hicks, A CONTRIBUTION TO THE THEORY OF THE TRADE CYCLE (London: Oxford University Press, 1950).

high propensity to fluctuate, cannot be effi-
ciently studied unless some of the variables are
lagged. . . . The easiest way to introduce lags
is to work in terms of period analysis._7/

Returning to our main theme, the instability
of the capitalist system has also been voiced by Professor Domar (1946-47)._8/ The Keynesian concern over
the insufficiency of investment is clearly stated by
Professor Domar in the following model:

(14) $\dfrac{dY_d}{dt} = \dfrac{1}{s} \dfrac{dI}{dt}$, where the subscript d
indicates aggregate demand.

(15) $\dfrac{dY_s}{dt} = \sigma I$, where the subscript s denotes
potential productive capacity.

(16) $\dfrac{dY_d}{dt} = \dfrac{dY_s}{dt}$

Equation (14) is the short-run income-
generating aspect of investment which is the same as
the Keynesian investment multiplier analysis. Equation (15) describes the capacity-creating aspect of
investment. The symbol σ may be viewed as the recip-
rocal of Harrod's β. The equation is derived in the
following way:

(17) $\dfrac{K}{Y} = \beta$

(18) $Y = \dfrac{1}{\beta} K = \sigma K$

_7/ J. R. Hicks, "Mr. Harrod's Dynamic Theory," ECO-
    NOMICA, May 1949, reprinted in READINGS IN BUSI-
    NESS CYCLES AND NATIONAL INCOME, edited by A. H.
    Hansen and R. V. Clemence (New York: W. W. Norton,
    1953), pp. 252-53.

_8/ E. D. Domar, "Capital Expansion, Rate of Growth
    and Employment," ECONOMETRICA, 1946, pp. 137-47,
    and "Expansion and Employment," AMERICAN ECONOMIC
    REVIEW, 1947, pp. 34-55.

$$(19) \quad \frac{dY_s}{dt} = \sigma \frac{dK}{dt} = \sigma I$$

Equation (16) is the equilibrium condition for steady-state growth. The required rate of investment to maintain equality between aggregate demand and potential productive capacity continuously over time is obtained by equating equation (14) with equation (15):

$$(20) \quad \frac{1}{s} \frac{dY}{dt} = \sigma I$$

$$(21) \quad \frac{1}{I} \frac{dI}{dt} = s\sigma .$$

The divergence between the actual rate of growth of investment and the required ("warranted") rate of investment is the "knife-edge" problem of Professor Domar. Although analytically the Domar model does not have an investment function, the central results of the Harrod and Domar models are similar. Since, as mentioned earlier in Chapter 1, it is the investment function which is of primary importance to the alternative approach to growth theory, Harrod's model may be more adequate in this respect.

References

Domar, E. D., "Capital Expansion, Rate of Growth and Employment," Econometrica, April 1946, pp. 137-47.

_____, "Expansion and Employment," American Economic Review, Vol. XXXVII, March 1947, pp. 34-55.

_____, ESSAYS IN THE THEORY OF GROWTH (London: Oxford University Press, 1957).

Harrod, R. F., THE TRADE CYCLE (London: Oxford University Press, 1936).

_____, "An Essay in Dynamic Theory," Economic Journal, Vol. XLIX, March 1939.

_____, TOWARDS A DYNAMIC ECONOMICS (London: Macmillan, 1948).

Hicks, J. R., A CONTRIBUTION TO THE THEORY OF THE TRADE CYCLE (Oxford: Oxford University Press, 1950).

_____, "Mr. Harrod's Dynamic Theory," Economica, Vol. 16, May 1949, pp. 106-21.

Kregel, J. A., RATE OF PROFIT, DISTRIBUTION AND GROWTH: TWO VIEWS (Chicago and New York: Aldine-Atherton, 1971).

Robinson, J., THE ACCUMULATION OF CAPITAL (Homewood, Ill.: Irwin, 1956).

Solow, R. M., "A Contribution to the Theory of Economic Growth," Quarterly Journal of Economics, Vol. 70, Feb. 1956.

CHAPTER 3

THEORETICAL HERITAGE OF THE

NEOCLASSICAL PARADIGM

The neoclassical paradigm in growth theory
stems from the so-called "marginal revolution" in the
1870's. Professor Blaug writes:

> The term "marginal revolution" is usually taken
> to refer to the nearly simultaneous but completely
> independent discovery in the early 1870's by
> Jevons, Menger, and Walras of the principle of
> diminishing marginal utility as the fundamental
> building block of a new kind of static micro-
> economics. 1/

It will be recalled that the "revolution" was
a revolt against the Ricardian theory of value and
distribution. Like other classical writers, Ricardo
was mainly concerned with economic growth. It was due
to his preoccupation with the growth process that he
was prompted to make a sharp distinction between those
commodities that could not be reproduced by the application of labor and raw materials, such as old masters' paintings, and those that were reproducible.
Clearly the first category of goods has nothing to do
with economic growth and the second category does.
Since he had no interest in the first category of
goods, Ricardo focused his attention solely on the

1/ Mark Blaug, "Was There a Marginal Revolution?"
in THE MARGINAL REVOLUTION IN ECONOMICS: INTERPRE-
TATION AND EVALUATION, edited by R. D. Collison
Black, A. W. Coats, and C. D. W. Goodwin (Durham:
Duke University Press, 1973), p. 3.

exchange value of the reproducible goods. _2/ His approach to the determination of the exchange value of reproducible goods highlighted the production process. Hence his value theory was in essence an objective real cost theory. In other words, prices are set so as to cover the technical cost of production. As pointed out by Professor E. J. Nell: "the Ricardian concept of exchange is irrevocably tied to the technological characteristics of the good involved; there is no exchange unless both items traded have a production equation." _3/

The marginalists saw the dichotomy of the Ricardian analysis and attempted to achieve a more unifying theory of value and distribution. In doing so they replaced the classical objective real cost theory of value with the more elegant neoclassical subjective value theory. The starting point of the new approach was the individual consumer's optimal decision-making under constraint. The entire theoretical framework was static equilibrium analysis. Subsequently, in the hands of Menger, Weiser, Wicksteed, and others, the entire economic process was cast in subjective terms. _4/ The concept of opportunity cost replaced the classical objective real cost

---

_2/ For a more detailed explanation of the Ricardian theory, the reader is requested to read Chapter 10 of this book.

_3/ E. J. Nell, "Theories of Growth and Theories of Value," in ECONOMIC DEVELOPMENT AND CULTURAL CHANGE, Vol. 16, 1967, pp. 15-26, reprinted in CAPITAL AND GROWTH, edited by G. C. Harcourt and N. F. Laing (Middlesex, England: Penguin Books, Ltd., 1971), p. 207.

_4/ For an excellent exposition of the "marginal

of production, for opportunity cost was considered
most relevant to the decision maker at the time of
making a rational choice. The counterpart of marginal utility was marginal productivity. Thus,
Professor Maurice Dobb observes:

> . . . the new orientation of economic analysis
> reduced the problem of distribution to the
> pricing of inputs by a market process which
> simultaneously determined the interconnected
> system of outputs and inputs. Moreover, not
> only was distribution . . . determined from
> within the market or exchange process, but in
> the form of the derived prices of given inter-
> mediate goods or productive factors: determina-
> tion was envisaged as being from the market for
> final products, and hence ultimately from the
> structure and intensity of consumers' demand. 5/

It should be noted that the subjective value
approach effectively removes: (a) the classical distinction between value and prices, (b) the classical
emphasis on the best utilization of the surplus for
economic growth, and (c) the priority of distribution
before value. "More importantly," writes Professor
J. A. Kregel, "it turns all output into old masters'
paintings by working with given supplies of goods and
given consumer incomes at a given point in time." 6/

---

revolution," see Mark Blaug, ECONOMIC THEORY IN
RETROSPECT, revised edition (Homewood, Ill.:
Richard D. Irwin, 1968), Chapters 8, 11, 12,
and 13.

5/ Maurice Dobb, THEORIES OF VALUE AND DISTRIBUTION
SINCE ADAM SMITH (London: Cambridge University
Press, 1973), p. 169.

6/ J. A. Kregel, THE RECONSTRUCTION OF POLITICAL
ECONOMY: AN INTRODUCTION TO POST-KEYNESIAN ECONOM-
ICS (New York: John Wiley & Sons, 1973), p. 28.
Prof. Kregel further writes: "The nomenclature of

The marginal revolution also gave birth to the powerful Walrasian general equilibrium analysis under static framework. It is powerful, because it provides an integrative intellectual framework for micro and macroeconomics. As mentioned earlier, the grand "neoclassical synthesis" is also based on Walrasian general equilibrium theory.

By the time of the so-called "Hicksian Revolution," 7/ the aesthetic sense of symmetry of the new approach had reached its peak. The elegant neoclassical theory is best described by Professor Ferguson as follows:

> There is basically one neoclassical theory embracing production, distribution, capital, and growth. . . . (it) is a beautiful edifice erected upon the foundations of microeconomic production functions (and input-output pricing processes). If these production functions, and the aggregate production derived from them, possess certain characteristics, the central results of neoclassical theory are obtained and the theory of production and distribution is validated. 8/

> the neoclassical theory--production, distribution, value--was the same as the Classical (recall the rabbit and the elephant) but their point of view was obviously different. Market prices were the sole point of reference in the explanation of why individuals made decisions about specific products and factors." Op. cit., p. 28.

7/ The so-called "Hicksian Revolution" took place when Sir John Hicks published his VALUE AND CAPITAL (London: Oxford University Press, 1939). It was an attempt by Sir John Hicks and R. G. D. Allen to change the whole technical face of microeconomics. They adopted the indifference-curves method (which was similar to "Occam's razor") to banish utilitarian philosophy from microeconomics.

8/ C. E. Ferguson, op. cit., p. 12.

The neoclassical theories of distribution and growth are clearly derivative theories, the former depending largely upon the theory of production, the latter upon capital theory. The theories of capital and production are more closely integrated and more fundamental. But in the last analysis neoclassical theory, in its simple and not-so-simple forms, depends upon the basic nature of the "thing" called capital. 9/

The central theorems of neoclassical theory are derived from the linearly homogeneous production function. Following Professor Ferguson, we may write the neoclassical system as follows:

$$(1) \quad y = f(k) \qquad f'(k) > 0 \qquad f''(k) < 0$$

Equation (1) is a linearly homogeneous production function permitting factor substitutability. The mathematical assumption of linear homogeneity amounts to the economic assumption of constant returns to scale. For linear homogeneity of degree one means that multiplying all inputs by λ increases output by λ also. That is to say, $\lambda Y = F(\lambda K, \lambda L)$. In per capita terms, this function may be written as: $\frac{Y}{L} = F(\frac{K}{L}, 1)$, or, simply as: $y = f(k)$, where $y \equiv \frac{Y}{L}$ and $k \equiv \frac{K}{L}$. Y stands for a single composite homogeneous output which can be transformed into either one unit of consumption good or one unit of capital good.

Equation (1) is the foundation of production theory. It stands or falls with the validity of the homogeneous K inserted in the bracket on the same footing as L. There were two strands of neoclassical thoughts in the theory of capital, namely, (a) the

_____

9/ C. E. Ferguson, op. cit., p. 251.

Austrian theory of capital and interest expounded by Eugen von Böhm-Bawerk (1851-1914), who adopted the concept of "average period of production" to justify the homogeneous capital in the neoclassical production function 10/; and (b) the real homogeneous capital model of the American economist John Bates Clark (1847-1938).11/ The homogeneous k in equation (1) follows the Clarkian concept. As mentioned earlier, here lies the source of the Cambridge controversies in the theory of capital, which will be discussed in Chapter 10 of this book.

$$(2) \quad f'(k) = r$$

where $f'(k)$ stands for the marginal product of capital and r denotes the rate of profit.

$$(3) \quad w = f(k) - f'(k)k$$

where w represents the real wage rate per man. Equation (3) may be used to illustrate the marginal productivity theory of distribution. We can rewrite equation (3) as: $f(k) = w + f'(k)k$, or, $y = w + rk$, which is the same as: $Y/L = w + r(K/L)$. If we multiply both sides of the preceding equation by L, we obtain:

$$(4) \quad Y = wL + rK.$$

Figure 1 is a graphical representation of the marginal productivity theory of distribution.

10/ See Mark Blaug, op. cit., Chapter 12, entitled: THE AUSTRIAN THEORY OF CAPITAL AND INTEREST.

11/ See C. E. Ferguson, op. cit., pp. 251-52.

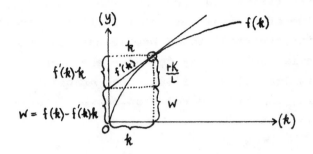

Figure 1

(5)   dr/dk = f"(k)

Equation (5) is one of the central theorems of neoclassical theory. It is one of Professor Harcourt's
"neoclassical parables."12/ This "parable" describes
the pattern of capital accumulation and economic
growth. Equation (5) states that there is an association between a lower rate of profit and higher
values of capital per man. Figures 2 and 3 depict
this particular relation.

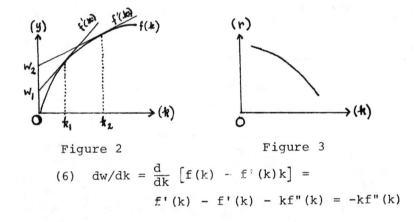

Figure 2   Figure 3

(6)   dw/dk = $\frac{d}{dk}$ $\left[f(k) - f'(k)k \right]$ =

$\quad\quad\quad\quad$ f'(k) - f'(k) - kf"(k) = -kf"(k)

12/ G. C. Harcourt, op. cit., p. 122.

29

Equation (6) depicts another "neoclassical parable," which ties the rising real wage per man with the increasing value of capital per man. It is just another way of stating the traditional belief that capital accumulation is the best way to raise the standard of living. This "parable" is illustrated graphically by Figure 4. The positive correlation between the two variables can also be seen in Figure 2.

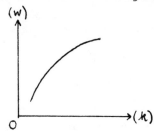

Figure 4

$$(7) \quad dw/dr = \frac{\dfrac{dw}{dk}}{\dfrac{dr}{dk}} = \frac{-kf''(k)}{f''(k)} = -k$$

Equation (7) states the slope of the factor-price frontier. Figure 5 is a graphical representation of equation (7).

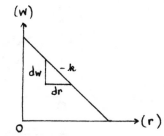

Figure 5

$$(8) \quad \frac{-\dfrac{dw}{w}}{\dfrac{dr}{r}} = -\left(\frac{dw}{dr}\right)\frac{r}{w} = -(-k)\frac{r}{w} = \left(\frac{K}{L}\right)\frac{r}{w} = \frac{rK}{wL}$$

30

The Marshallian elasticity of the factor-price frontier is the ratio of aggregate factor shares. Equation (8) describes this ratio and we are back to the marginal productivity theory of distribution again.

The expression for the factor-price frontier (wage-capital rental ratio) is equation (9):

$$(9) \quad \frac{w}{r} = \frac{f(k) - f'(k)k}{f'(k)} = \frac{f(k)}{f'(k)} - k$$

Figure 6 is a graphical illustration of equation (9).

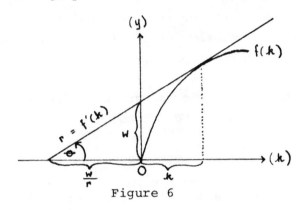

Figure 6

It is interesting to note that, because the neoclassical theory is built on the foundation of the linearly homogeneous production function, all relevant variables are dependent functions of the capital-labor ratio (k). The nine equations mentioned above are forceful testimonies of this assertion. Furthermore, savings per man, capital-widening, and capital-deepening are all functions of the capital-labor, or capital per man, ratio. These relations are described by the following three equations:

$$(10) \quad S/L = I/L = sf(k) = sY/L$$

where s denotes the constant savings ratio.

(11) $\dot{K}/K = n$, or, $\dot{K} = nK$, or,

$I/L = nk = sf(k)$.

> This is capital widening, or the "golden-age" rate of capital accumulation.

(12) $\dot{k} = sf(k) - nk$, or, $\dot{k} = \emptyset(k)$.

> This equation describes capital deepening, or increases in the capital per man ratio.

Thus, a one-sector neoclassical growth model can be constructed by introducing the neoclassical linearly homogeneous production function. This is illustrated by Professor Solow's model. A short introduction to the Solovian growth model is the subject matter of the following Chapter 4.

References

Blaug, M., ECONOMIC THEORY IN RETROSPECT, revised edition (Homewood, Ill.: Irwin, 1968).

_____, "Was There a Marginal Revolution?" in THE MARGINAL REVOLUTION IN ECONOMICS: INTERPRETATION AND EVALUATION, edited by R. D. Collison Black, A. W. Coats, and C. D. W. Goodwin (Durham: Duke University Press, 1973).

Dobb, M. H., THEORIES OF VALUE AND DISTRIBUTION SINCE ADAM SMITH (London: Cambridge University Press, 1973).

Ferguson, C. E., THE NEOCLASSICAL THEORY OF PRODUCTION AND DISTRIBUTION (Great Britain: Cambridge University Press, 1969).

Harcourt, G. C., and N. F. Laing, editors, CAPITAL AND GROWTH (Middlesex, England: Penguin Books, Ltd., 1971).

Hicks, J. R., VALUE AND CAPITAL (London: Oxford University Press, 1939).

Kregel, J. A., THE RECONSTRUCTION OF POLITICAL
ECONOMY: AN INTRODUCTION TO POST-KEYNESIAN
ECONOMICS (New York: John Wiley & Sons,
1973).

Nell, E. J., "Theories of Growth and Theories of
Value," Economic Development and Cultural
Change, Vol. 16, 1967, pp. 15-26.

CHAPTER 4

THE BASIC NEOCLASSICAL MODEL

WITHOUT TECHNICAL PROGRESS

It will be recalled that the Harrodian "knife edge" problem stems from the rigidities of the three key parameters: s, β, and n. To maintain "golden age" growth, one of the three parameters has to be flexible. The Solovian model makes β flexible by introducing the linearly homogeneous production function into the Harrodian formulation. The basic Solovian model may be written as follows:

$$(1) \quad \dot{K} = sY$$

Although equation (1) is similar to that of Harrod's model, the sequence of causality is quite different. Whereas Harrod follows Keynes, who stood the traditional neoclassical proposition on its head by making savings follow investment, Professor Solow, on the other hand, follows the neoclassical tradition. It should be noted, however, that the intent of the neoclassical model is not to restore Say's law. The neoclassicism is justified by the Samuelsonian concept of the grand "neoclassical synthesis."

$$(2) \quad L = L_o e^{nt}$$

This is the same equation which appears in Harrod's model.

$$(3) \quad Y = F(K,L)$$

Equation (3) introduces the neoclassical production

function into the model.

$$(4) \quad \dot{K} = sF(K, L_o e^{nt})$$

Equation (4) is obtained by substituting equations (2) and (3) into (1). This equation states the time path that capital accumulation must follow if the growing labor force is to remain fully employed.

$$(5) \quad K = kL$$

Equation (5) is simply another way of writing the definitional equation of the capital-labor ratio. Substituting equation (2) into (5), one has:

$$(6) \quad K = kL_o e^{nt}$$

Differentiating equation (6) with respect to time, t, yields:

$$(7) \quad \dot{K} = knL_o e^{nt} + L_o e^{nt} \dot{k}$$

Substituting equation (4) into (7), one obtains:

$$(8) \quad sF(K, L_o e^{nt}) = knL_o e^{nt} + L_o e^{nt} \dot{k}$$

Next, we divide both sides of equation (8) by the expression $L_o e^{nt}$ to obtain:

$$(9) \quad sF \left(\frac{K}{L_o e^{nt}}, 1 \right) = nk + \dot{k}$$

The fundamental equation of the Solovian model is obtained by rewriting equation (9) as:

$$(10) \quad \dot{k} = sf(k) - nk.$$

The fundamental equation is a differential equation expressed in a single variable k. It has two parameters, namely, s and n. Figure 7 is a graphical representation of equation (10).

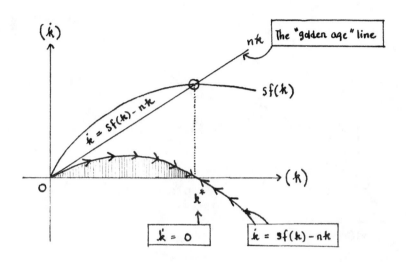

Figure 7

The dynamic process of attaining the golden-age growth path is described by the phase line in Figure 7. The phase line must cross the horizontal axis at point k*. The vertical distance between the phase line and the horizontal axis (the shaded area) is identical with the vertical distance between sf(k) and nk.

Alternatively, the basic Solovian model may be depicted by Figure 8, which brings the linearly homogeneous production function in per capita terms into the diagram. The vertical axis of Figure 8 measures y, or output per man, and the horizontal axis measures k, which is the same as in Figure 7.

37

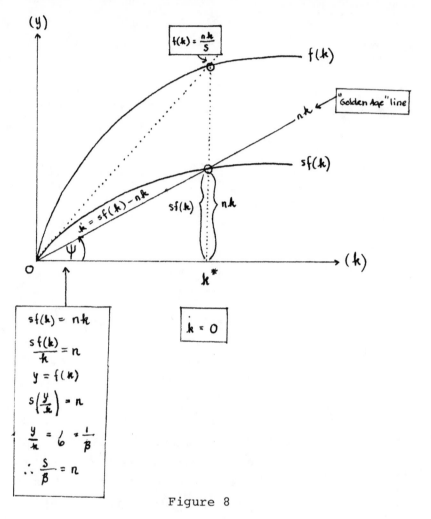

Figure 8

We prefer to call the nk line the "golden age" line, for it is the locus of all possible "golden age" points, or "sf(k) = nk" points. It is analogous to the 45 degree line in the static Keynesian-cross diagram.

The point k* is a stable and unique "golden age" point, if the production function is well-behaved as depicted by Figure 8. However, the necessary and sufficient conditions for the existence, uniqueness, and stability of the steady-state k* also require the following Inada "derivative conditions": 1/

(i) $f'(0) = \infty$ (That is to day that the marginal product of capital is infinite when k approaches zero.)

(ii) $f'(\infty) = 0$ (This condition means that, when k increases indefinitely, the marginal product of capital falls to zero.)

These two "derivative conditions" are the boundary conditions restricting the attainable values of k. For these specifications assure that k̇ will be positive before k reaches k* and that k̇ becomes negative when k increases beyond k*.

Conceivably, multiple equilibria are possible if the parameters s and n become endogenous themselves. Panel (a) of Figure 9 describes a possible growth pattern when the savings ratio is an endogenous variable. Panel (b) illustrates another possible growth pattern when the growth rate of the labor force is an endogenous variable.

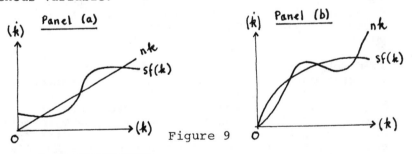

Figure 9

1/ See K. Inada, "On a Two-Sector Model of Economic Growth: Comments and a Generalization," REVIEW OF ECONOMIC STUDIES, Vol. 30, June 1963, pp. 119-127.

The one-sector neoclassical growth model has been criticized by writers of Cambridge, England. The following are a few salient points of their criticisms:

(1) The investment function is absent from the neoclassical model. For the model implicitly assumes that savings automatically lead to investment. Thus, Professor Joan Robinson calls the neoclassical model "pre-Keynesian theory after Keynes." 2/

(2) The neoclassical model assumes malleability of capital which eliminates historical time. For the assumption implies that mistakes in investment decisions can always be undone and an equilibrium is, therefore, always assured. 3/

(3) The marginal productivity theory of distribution is untenable. This is one of the important issues in the Cambridge controversies concerning the theory of capital which will be discussed in Chapter 11 of this volume.

Figure 10 is a graphical illustration of these three criticisms:

2/ Joan Robinson, "Pre-Keynesian Theory After Keynes," in COLLECTED ECONOMIC PAPERS, Vol. 3 (Oxford, England: Oxford University Press, 1965), pp. 56-69.

3/ Joan Robinson, "The Second Crisis of Economic Theory," op. cit. Professor Robinson observes in that lecture: "The strangest of all is to set up a model of a one-commodity world where there are no prices, saving governs investment, full employment is guaranteed by the real wage rate, the difference between the future and the past is eliminated by making capital 'malleable' so that mistakes can always be undone and equilibrium is always guaranteed . . ."

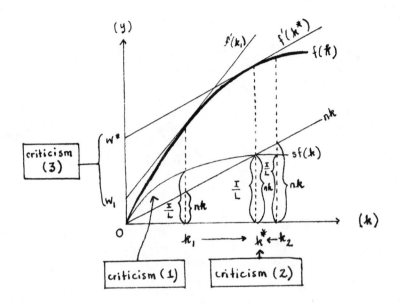

Figure 10

References

Inada, K., "On a Two-Sector Model of Economic Growth: Comments and a Generalization," Review of Economic Studies, Vol. XXX, June 1963.

Robinson, J., COLLECTED ECONOMIC PAPERS, Vol. 3 (Oxford: Oxford University Press, 1965).

Solow, R. M., "A Contribution to the Theory of Economic Growth," Quarterly Journal of Economics, Vol. 70, Feb. 1956.

_____, GROWTH THEORY: AN EXPOSITION (New York and Oxford: Oxford University Press, 1970).

Swan, T. W., "Economic Growth and Capital Accumulation," Economic Record, Vol. XXXII, Nov. 1956.

CHAPTER 5

THE BASIC NEOCLASSICAL MODEL WITH

DISEMBODIED TECHNICAL PROGRESS

The existence of "golden age" growth in the
neoclassical growth model requires disembodied Harrod-
neutral technical progress. By disembodied, it is
meant that technical progress can occur in the absence
of gross investment. Such technical progress applies
alike to all capital and labor in current use. It is
organizational in the sense that its effect on productivity does not require any change in the quantity
of inputs. By Harrod-neutral technical progress, it
is meant that "at a constant rate of interest, [the
technical progress] does not disturb the value of the
capital coefficient" and "leave[s] the distribution
of the total national product as between labour (in
the broadest sense) and capital unchanged." 1/ Furthermore, Harrod-neutral technical progress is labor-
augmenting in the sense that it is tantamount to a
corresponding increase in the labor force. In other
words, it enables one man to do twice, or thrice (and
so on), as much work as he did before the technical
progress.

Constant relative shares implies that the
elasticity of substitution is unity. This proposition

1/ R. F. Harrod, TOWARDS A DYNAMIC ECONOMICS (London:
   Macmillan, 1956), pp. 22-23. The words in
   brackets are ours.

may be demonstrated as follows:

(1) Let $\theta = \dfrac{rK}{wL}$; $\lambda = \dfrac{r}{w}$; and $k = K/L$.

We can write:

(2) $\theta = \lambda k$

(3) $\ln\theta = \ln\lambda + \ln k$

(4) $\dfrac{\dot\theta}{\theta} = \dfrac{\dot\lambda}{\lambda} + \dfrac{\dot k}{k} = 0$ [constancy]

(5) $\dfrac{\dot\lambda}{\lambda} = \dfrac{-\dot k}{k}$

(6) $\dot\lambda k = -\dot k \lambda$

(7) $\dfrac{\dot\lambda k}{\dot\lambda k} = 1 = -\dfrac{\dot k \lambda}{\dot\lambda k} = -\dfrac{\left(\dfrac{\dot k}{k}\right)}{\left(\dfrac{\dot\lambda}{\lambda}\right)} = b$ [elasticity of substitution]

The Cobb-Douglas production function has this property. Furthermore, it is linearly homogeneous and may, therefore, be written in any of the following three forms:

(i) $Y = Ae^{mt}K^a L^{1-a}$,

(ii) $Y = A\left[e^{\frac{m}{a}t} K\right]^a L^{1-a}$,

(iii) $Y = AK^a\left[e^{\frac{m}{1-a}t} L\right]^{1-a}$.

The term Ae^{mt} represents the index of disembodied technical progress at time t, where disembodied technical progress grows at the constant rate m. The exponents a and (1-a) stand for capital's relative share of total income and that of labor, respectively. This follows directly from the marginal productivity theory of distribution, for partial differentiation of the production function with respect to K yields the marginal product of capital:

44

$$(8) \quad \frac{\partial Y}{\partial K} = Ae^{mt}aK^{a-1}L^{1-a} = \frac{a\left[Ae^{mt}K^aL^{1-a}\right]}{K} = a\,\frac{Y}{K}$$

Rearranging equation (8), one obtains the relative income share of capital:

$$(9) \quad \frac{\partial Y}{\partial K} \cdot K = aY . \qquad \therefore a = \frac{\frac{\partial Y}{\partial K} \cdot K}{Y}$$

Similarly, partial differentiation of the production function with respect to L yields the marginal product of labor:

$$(10) \quad \frac{\partial Y}{\partial L} = Ae^{mt}K^a(1-a)L^{1-a-1} = (1-a)\frac{Y}{L} .$$

$$\therefore (1-a) = \frac{\frac{\partial Y}{\partial L} \cdot L}{Y}$$

Rearranging equation (10), the relative income share of labor is obtained.

Harrod-neutral labor-augmenting technical progress is represented by equation (iii). It should be noted that in equation (iii) the labor input is measured in efficiency units, i.e., $e^{\frac{m}{1-a}t}L$, instead of the natural units, L.

Equation (i) is the Cobb-Douglas production function incorporating Hicks-neutral technical progress, 2/ and equation (ii) incorporates Solow-neutral technical progress in the production function. 3/ Solow-neutral technical progress is capital-augmenting, which is most relevant to vintage models in which technical progress is embodied in successive vintages of machines that become more efficient over time.

2/ See J. R. Hicks, THE THEORY OF WAGES (New York: Macmillan, 1932).

3/ See Robert M. Solow, CAPITAL THEORY AND THE RATE OF RETURN (Chicago: Rand-McNally, 1963).

The basic neoclassical growth model incorporating Harrod-neutral technical progress may now be stated as follows:

(11) $Y = Ae^{mt}K^aL^{1-a}$

Differentiating equation (11) with respect to time, t, one obtains:

(12) $\dfrac{dY}{dt} = mY + a\dfrac{Y}{K}\dfrac{dK}{dt} + (1-a)\dfrac{Y}{L}\dfrac{dL}{dt}$

Next, to derive the percentage rates of growth of Y, K, and L, one divides both sides of equation (12) by Y:

(13) $\dfrac{\dot{Y}}{Y} = m + a\dfrac{\dot{K}}{K} + (1-a)\dfrac{\dot{L}}{L}$

Equation (13) shows three separate sources of economic growth, namely, m, $\dfrac{\dot{K}}{K}$, and $\dfrac{\dot{L}}{L}$. Since the rate of growth of the labor force is still assumed to be the same constant rate, n, the last term may be written as: $(1-a)n$.

"Golden age" growth requires:

(14) $\dfrac{\dot{Y}}{Y} = \dfrac{\dot{K}}{K}$

Hence, one may substitute $\dfrac{\dot{Y}}{Y}$ for $\dfrac{\dot{K}}{K}$ in equation (13):

(15) $\dfrac{\dot{Y}}{Y} = m + a\dfrac{\dot{Y}}{Y} + (1-a)n$

Rearranging terms, we have:

(16) $\dfrac{\dot{Y}}{Y} = \dfrac{m}{1-a} + n$

Equation (16) can be transformed to show the percentage rate of growth of output per man, $\dfrac{\dot{y}}{y}$:

(17) $\dfrac{\dot{y}}{y} = \dfrac{\dot{Y}}{Y} - n = \dfrac{m}{1-a}$

Next, one substitutes $\dfrac{\dot{K}}{K}$ for $\dfrac{\dot{Y}}{Y}$ in equation (13):

(18) $\dfrac{\dot{K}}{K} = m + a\dfrac{\dot{K}}{K} + (1-a)n$

46

Rearranging terms, one has:

(19) $\dfrac{\dot{K}}{K} = \dfrac{m}{1-a} + n$

The equation for the percentage rate of growth of capital per man can be written as:

(20) $\dfrac{\dot{k}}{k} = \dfrac{\dot{K}}{K} - n = \dfrac{m}{1-a}$

It should be noted that with labor-augmenting technical progress indicated by the term m/1-a, both output per man and capital per man can rise beyond the limitation imposed by the rate of growth of the labor force. This assertion is illustrated by equations (17) and (20). If $\dfrac{m}{1-a} = 0$, then $\dfrac{\dot{y}}{y} = n$ and $\dfrac{\dot{k}}{k} = n$. The rise in both the equilibrium y* and the equilibrium k* is obviously due to the labor-augmenting technical progress, which enables the same man at time t to do two (or more) times as much work as he did originally. Figure 11 describes the basic neoclassical growth model incorporating disembodied Harrod-neutral technical progress.

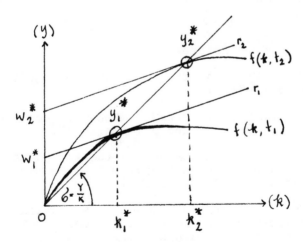

Figure 11

The real wage rate, w, is shown in Figure 11 to rise at the same rates of growth as y and k. This point may be illustrated as follows:

$$(21) \quad w = (1-a)\frac{Y}{L}$$

Equation (21) is simply the condition for equilibrium factor-hire under perfect competition, namely, the real wage rate is equal to the marginal product of labor. Since, in the present case, $\frac{\dot{Y}}{Y} = \frac{m}{1-a} + n$ and $\frac{\dot{L}}{L} = n$, one may substitute these two expressions into equation (21) to obtain:

$$(22) \quad w = (1-a)\frac{Y_o e^{(\frac{m}{1-a} + n)t}}{L_o e^{nt}}$$

which may be rewritten as:

$$(23) \quad w = (1-a)\frac{Y_o}{L_o} e^{\frac{m}{1-a}t}$$

Equation (23) indicates that both the real wage rate and the marginal product of labor grow at the constant rate of $\frac{m}{1-a}$.

References

Harrod, R. F., TOWARDS A DYNAMIC ECONOMICS (London: Macmillan, 1956).

Hicks, J. R., THE THEORY OF WAGES (London: Macmillan, 1st edition 1932, 2nd edition 1963).

Solow, R. M., "Technical Change and the Aggregate Production Function," Review of Economic Studies, Vol. 39, Aug. 1957.

_____, "Technical Progress, Capital Formation, and Economic Growth," American Economic Review, Papers and Proceedings, Vol. L 11, May 1962.

_____, CAPITAL THEORY AND THE RATE OF RETURN (Chicago: Rand-McNally, 1963).

CHAPTER 6

THE BASIC NEOCLASSICAL MODEL WITH

EMBODIED TECHNICAL PROGRESS

In an important theoretical paper, Professor
Solow has shown that the neoclassical aggregate production function and the aggregate homogeneous capital
in it can be modified to accommodate machines of different vintages. 1/ The necessary and sufficient conditions for the aggregation of heterogeneous capital
have been subsequently given by Professor Fisher as
follows: 2/

(a) linearly homogeneous production function
for every industry;

(b) capital-augmenting technical progress
everywhere; and

(c) optimal allocation of the labor force so
that the marginal product of labor is the same for all
vintages of capital equipment in existence.

The vintage model that satisfies these conditions has been called the "putty-putty" case. For
there is substitution between machines and labor at

1/ R. M. Solow, "Investment and Technical Progress,"
in MATHEMATICAL METHODS IN THE SOCIAL SCIENCES,
1959, edited by K. J. Arrow, S. Karlin, and P.
Suppes (Stanford, California: Stanford University
Press, 1960), Chapter 7.

2/ F. M. Fisher, "Embodied Technical Change and the
Existence of an Aggregate Capital Stock," THE
REVIEW OF ECONOMIC STUDIES, Vol. 32, October
1965, pp. 263-287.

all times--at and after installation--according to the same Cobb-Douglas production function. Furthermore, labor is allocated to different vintages of machines under perfect competition. Less labor is allocated to older machines than to new machines. Thus the question of scrapping old machines does not arise. Hence, the putty-putty case is analogous to the Ricardian theory of differential rent. Machines of different vintages are like plots of land with different productivity; and the allocation of labor similarly has both an extensive and an intensive margin. It should also be noted that is is gross investment in new machines which is relevant to the vintage models; whereas in the case of disembodied technical progress it is net investment that is relevant to the analysis of homogeneous capital stock.

A simply "putty-putty" model is discussed in the following sections. The analysis follows Professor Solow's model.

$$(1) \quad Y_{(v,t)} = Ae^{\lambda v}K^{\alpha}_{(v,t)}L^{1-a}_{(v,t)}$$

Equation (1) satisfies conditions (a) and (b) above. It is linearly homogeneous in the Cobb-Douglas form with capital-augmenting technical progress. In this case, one needs two time variables: one for time denoted by t in the usual sense, and the other v for the dating of vintages of machines in use at time t. Equation (1) shows that output $Y_{(v,t)}$ is produced by labor $L_{(v,t)}$ employed on capital of vintage v at current time period t; i.e., $K_{(v,t)}$. It follows that total output from all employed vintages of capital equipment can be written as:

$$(2) \quad Y_t = \int_{-\infty}^{t} Y_{(v,t)} dv$$

$$(3) \quad M_t = \frac{\partial Y_{(v,t)}}{\partial L_{(v,t)}} = Ae^{\lambda v} K^a_{(v,t)} (1-a)L^{-a}_{(v,t)}$$

Equation (3) satisfies condition (c) above. M_t stands
for the uniform marginal product of labor under perfect competition, which is derived by partially
differentiating equation (1) with respect to L.
Rearranging terms one obtains:

$$(4) \quad L^{-a}_{(v,t)} = (1-a)^{-1} A^{-1} e^{-\lambda v} K^{-a}_{(v,t)} M_t$$

Dividing the exponents by -a yields:

$$(5) \quad L_{(v,t)} = (1-a)^{\frac{1}{a}} A^{\frac{1}{a}} e^{\frac{\lambda v}{a}} K^{\frac{-a}{-a}}_{(v,t)} M_t^{-\frac{1}{a}}$$

$$(6) \quad \text{Let } h_t = (1-a)^{\frac{1}{a}} A^{\frac{1}{a}} M_t^{-\frac{1}{a}}$$

Equation (5) can then be rewritten as:

$$(7) \quad L_{(v,t)} = h_t e^{\frac{\lambda v}{a}} K_{(v,t)}$$

From equation (7), by definite integration, the total
labor force employed is derived:

$$(8) \quad L_t = h_t \int_{-\infty}^{t} e^{\frac{\lambda v}{a}} K_{(v,t)} \, dv$$

$$(9) \quad \text{Let } J_t = \int_{-\infty}^{t} e^{\frac{\lambda v}{a}} K_{(v,t)} \, dv$$

where J_t stands for the effective capital stock, or
productivity adjusted capital stock weighted by the
productivity improvement factor $e^{\frac{\lambda v}{a}}$. For older
capital stock, v becomes smaller. Thus, heterogeneous
capital equipment in existence has finally been aggre-
gated. To recapitulate, the aggregation is made possible by satisfying the three Fisherian necessary and
sufficient conditions.

Substituting equation (9) into (8), we obtain:

(10) $\quad L_t = h_t J_t$, or, (10') $\quad h_t = L_t J_t^{-1}$

Next, we substitute equation (7) into equation (1) to obtain:

(11) $\quad Y_{(v,t)} = Ae^{\lambda v} K_{(v,t)}^a \left[h_t \; e^{\frac{\lambda v}{a}} \; K_{(v,t)} \right]^{1-a} =$

$$Ae^{\lambda v} K_{(v,t)}^a \; h_t^{1-a} \; e^{\frac{\lambda v (1-a)}{a}} \; K_{(v,t)}^{1-a}$$

Rearranging terms yields:

(12) $\quad Y_{(v,t)} = Ae^{\frac{\lambda v}{a}} \; h_t^{1-a} \; K_{(v,t)}$

Substituting equation (12) into equation (2), we have:

(13) $\quad Y_t = A \; h_t^{1-a} \int_{-\infty}^{t} e^{\frac{\lambda v}{a}} \; K_{(v,t)} \; dv$

The purpose of the preceding operation is to derive the modified neoclassical aggregate production function. Since $J_t = \int_{-\infty}^{t} e^{\frac{\lambda v}{a}} K_{(v,t)} \; dv$, equation (13) can be rewritten as:

(14) $\quad Y_t = A \; h_t^{1-a} \; J_t = A \left[L_t J_t^{-1} \right]^{1-a} J_t =$

$$A \; L_t^{1-a} \; J_t^{a-1+1}$$

Rearranging terms, one finally reaches the destination:

(15) $\quad Y_t = A \; J_t^a \; L_t^{1-a}$

Equation (15) is the modified neoclassical aggregate production function. J_t , the effective capital stock, now replaces the homogeneous K of "J. B. Clark's fairy tale." Furthermore, the new theory also does away with the thorny problem of

measuring K. Thus, the new view of investment is a
partial answer to Professor Joan Robinson's criticisms.

References

Fisher, F., "Embodied Technology and the Existence of
an Aggregate Capital Stock," Review of Economic Studies, Vol. XXXII, 1965.

_____, "Embodied Technology and the Aggregation of
Fixed and Movable Capital Goods," Review of
Economic Studies, Vol. XXXV, Oct. 1968.

Solow, R. M., "Investment and Technical Progress," in
MATHEMATICAL METHODS IN THE SOCIAL SCIENCES,
1959, K. J. Arrow, S. Karlin, and P. Suppes,
eds. (Stanford, California: Stanford University Press, 1960).

_____, "Heterogeneous Capital and Smooth Production
Functions: An Experimental Study," Econometrica, Vol. 31, Oct. 1963.

CHAPTER 7

THE ROLE OF MONEY IN THE BASIC

NEOCLASSICAL MODEL

The one-sector, one asset, neoclassical growth
model has been generalized to include the monetary
sector by Tobin, Johnson, Levhari and Patinkin, Sidrauski, Shaw, Solow and others. 1/ The simple model
discussed in this chapter is centered around the
Levhari-Patinkin model.

An outstanding feature of the neoclassical
growth model including the monetary sector is that
wealth may now be held in alternative forms, namely,
physical capital, K, or real money balances, M/P.
For simplicity's sake, money in the present case is
assumed to be purely of the "outside" variety (govern-
ment debt). Uncertainty and risks involved in financial decisions are also abstracted from our present
consideration. Symbolically, the wealth equation can
be written as:

(1) $W = K + M/P$.

A second distinguishing feature of the model
with two assets is that the savings decision (which
is the only explicit decision variable in the one-
asset model) has now been supplemented by a portfolio
decision. Consequently, in any steady-state growth
path, two conditions have to be simultaneously

1/ See references at the end of this chapter.

satisfied: (a) the "golden age" condition discussed
in chapter 2, and (b) an additional "portfolio balance" condition which assures the continuous equilibrium in the money and capital market.

The real stock of money, according to Professors Levhari and Patinkin, has two important functions.
In the first place, it yields "utility" or the flow of
"convenient services" to its holders. In this sense,
real balances are equivalent to a consumption good.
Secondly, the real stock of money may be considered
as an additional input in the linearly homogeneous
production function. With money, producers would
not have to divert resources to search for the "double
coincidence" of barter. "Hence the entrance of money
into the production function reflects the fact that
it frees labor and capital for the production of commodities proper. This is an alternative expression of
the greater specialization and exchange which money
makes possible." 2/ In the second sense, real balances may be treated as a production good. Professors
Levhari and Patinkin analyze money service as a consumption good and as a production good separately.
We shall follow their procedure by discussing the
implications of money service as a consumption good
first. Then the implications of money service as a
production good will be considered.

Money Service as a Consumption Good

When money is treated as a consumption good,
the definition of disposable income to society should
be augmented by including not only the increment of

2/ Levhari and Patinkin, op. cit., p. 738.

"outside money" in real terms but also the service of real cash balances held by consumers. In a barter economy with one asset, disposable social income is limited to the national product, $Y = F(K,L)$. In a monetary economy with two assets, disposable social income is defined as follows:

$$(2) \quad Yd = Y + \frac{d}{dt}\frac{M}{P} + \frac{M}{P}(r+\pi) =$$
$$F(K,L) + \frac{d}{dt}\frac{M}{P} + \frac{M}{P}(r+\pi)$$

where Yd denotes disposable social income; Y represents net national product; $\frac{d}{dt}\frac{M}{P}$ stands for the increment in the stock of real "outside money"; r is the real rate or own-rate of return on capital ($r = f'(k) = \frac{\partial Y}{\partial K}$); and the expected rate of change in the price level is symbolized by π. The expression $i = r+\pi$ means that the nominal or money rate of interest is equal to the real rate plus the expected rate of change in prices; thus the expression $\frac{M}{P}(r+\pi)$ indicates the service of money as a consumption good, for i may be considered as the opportunity cost of holding real balances.

The expression $\frac{d}{dt}\frac{M}{P}$ can be rewritten as $\frac{M}{P}(\mu+\pi)$ where μ stands for the percentage rate of change in the nominal stock of "outside money," $\frac{\dot{M}}{M}$. The new expression is derived in the following way:

$$\frac{d}{dt}(\frac{M}{P}) = \frac{P\frac{dM}{dt} - M\frac{dP}{dt}}{P^2} = \frac{1}{P}\frac{dM}{dt} - \frac{M}{P^2}\frac{dP}{dt}$$

$$= \frac{1}{P}(\frac{M}{M})\frac{dM}{dt} - \frac{M}{P}(\frac{1}{P})\frac{dP}{dt} = \frac{M}{P}\frac{1}{M}\frac{dM}{dt} - \frac{M}{P}\frac{1}{P}\frac{dP}{dt}$$

$$= \frac{M}{P}\left[\frac{1}{M}\frac{dM}{dt} - \frac{1}{P}\frac{dP}{dt}\right] = \frac{M}{P}\left[\frac{\dot{M}}{M} - \frac{\dot{P}}{P}\right]$$

$$= \frac{M}{P}(\mu-\pi) .$$

Substituting the derived expression into equation (2), we have:

(3) $Yd = Y + \frac{M}{P}(\mu+r)$

The real disposable social income determines the consumption (savings) behavior of individuals. We can write:

(4) $Y_Q = C + S$

In a monetary economy not all savings are devoted to capital accumulation; instead, some savings can be diverted to the accumulation of real balances. Thus we can write:

(5) $S = Sp + \frac{d}{dt}\frac{M}{P}$, or,

(5') $Sp \therefore I \equiv \dot{K} = S - \frac{d}{dt}\frac{M}{P}$

Both equation (5) and equation (5') imply that real balances and physical investment compete for total savings, S. $Sp = I = \dot{K}$ stands for physical savings; whereas $\frac{d}{dt}\frac{M}{P}$ signifies money savings.

In a similar vein, total consumption, C, also has two components, namely, physical consumption, Cp, and consumption of liquidity services, $\frac{M}{P}(r+\pi)$. This notion is depicted by the following equation:

(6) $C = Cp + \frac{M}{P}(r+\pi)$

Combining equations (3), (4), and (6), we obtain:

(7) $Cp = (1-s)\left[F(K,L) + \frac{M}{P}(\mu+r)\right] - \frac{M}{P}(r+\pi)$

where total consumption is represented by the expression $(1-s)\left[F(K,L) + \frac{M}{P}(\mu+r)\right]$; the symbol s stands for the constant propensity to save; (1-s) is the constant propensity to consume.

58

The source of capital accumulation is physical savings. The equation for capital accumulation can be written as:

$$(8) \quad \dot{K} = F(K,L) - \{(1-s)\left[F(K,L) + \frac{M}{P}(\mu+r)\right] - \frac{M}{P}(r+\pi)\}$$

The notion that capital accumulation is a substitute for holding real money balances is implied by the last term, $-\frac{M}{P}(r+\pi)$. It should also be noted that the aforementioned equation pertains to the savings decision of the community.

Turning now to the portfolio decision of the community, we have to consider money-market conditions. In their treatment of the money market, Professors Levhari and Patinkin follow the classical tradition of monetary theory and make use of the assumption of wage-price flexibility and automatic adjustment of the demand for real balances to their supply. They further assume that the demand for real balances, $\frac{M^d}{P}$, bears a fixed proportion, λ, to national product. The equilibrium condition for the money market is shown by the following equation:

$$(9) \quad \frac{M^d}{P} = \lambda Y = \lambda F(K,L) = \frac{M^S}{P}$$

where the symbol $\frac{M^S}{P}$ stands for the supply of real balances. Whereas the nominal quantity of money, M, is treated as an exogenous variable, real balances $\frac{M}{P}$ are considered to be a strategic endogenous variable. The desired level of real balances in per capita terms is $\frac{M}{PL}$ which is assumed to be a function of the level of per capita real income, $y = f(k)$, the expected own-rate of return on capital, r_e, and the expected return on real balances, which is the negative of the expected

rate of change in prices $(-\frac{\dot{Pe}}{P} = -\pi)$. Portfolio
balance for the community as a whole requires that
the real expected rates of return on the two assets
be equal. For simplicity, however, Professors Levhari
and Patinkin assume that the expected or anticipated
rates are always equal to the existing rates.

Substituting equation (9) into (8), we have:

(10) $\dot{K} = Y - \{(1-s)\left[Y + \lambda(\mu+r)Y\right] - \lambda(r+\pi)Y\}$

In doing so, we have brought the savings decision and the portfolio decision together. Now we
have to consider the steady-state conditions for the
two-asset model. It will be recalled that each
steady-state growth path is characterized by its constant capital labor ratio (k) in the one-sector and
one-asset growth model. However, in the two-asset
model, each steady-state growth path is characterized
by both its constant capital-labor ratio and its constant money-labor ratio (real-balances per man), M/PL.

The constancy of the capital-labor ratio
along the steady-state growth path is symbolized by
the following equation:

(11) $\frac{\dot{k}}{k} = \frac{\dot{K}}{K} - \frac{\dot{L}}{L} = \frac{\dot{K}}{K} - n = 0$, or

(11') $\frac{\dot{K}}{K} = n$

where the symbol n, as explained before in chapter 3,
is the exogenously determined growth rate of the labor
force, which, in the steady-state, is also equal to
the natural rate of growth of aggregate output
$(\frac{\dot{Y}}{Y} = \frac{\dot{K}}{K} = n)$.

Let $m = \frac{M}{PL}$. The constancy of the money-labor
ratio along the steady-state growth path can be

60

characterized as follows:

$$(12) \quad \frac{\dot{m}}{m} = \frac{\dot{M}}{M} - \frac{\dot{P}}{P} - \frac{\dot{L}}{L} = \mu - \pi - n = 0 \ , \ \text{or}$$

$$(12') \quad \pi = \mu - n$$

Equation (12') implies that in a steady-state the rate of inflation must be constant and that it must be equal to the difference between the rate of growth of the money supply and the natural rate of growth of output per man.

Making use of equations (11') and (12'), equation (10) can be rewritten as:

$$(13) \quad \dot{K} = F(K,L) \ \{s\left[1+\lambda(n+\pi+r)\right] - \lambda n\} \quad \underline{3/}$$

Dividing equation (13) through by K, we obtain:

$$(14) \quad \frac{\dot{K}}{K} = \frac{F(K,L)}{K} \ \{s\left[1+\lambda(n+\pi+r)\right] - \lambda n\}$$

$\underline{3/}$ The derivation of equation (13) is as follows:

(a) $\quad \dot{K} = Y - \{(1-s)\left[Y+\frac{M}{P}(\mu+r)\right] - \frac{M}{P}(r+\pi)\}$

(b) $\quad \dot{K} = Y - \{(1-s)\left[Y+\lambda(\mu+r)Y\right] - \lambda(r+\pi)Y\}$

(c) $\quad \dot{K} = Y\{1-(1-s)\left[1+\lambda(\mu+r)\right] + \lambda(r+\pi)\}$

(d) $\quad \dot{K} = Y\{1-\left[(1-s)+\lambda(\mu+r) - s\lambda(\mu+r)\right] + \lambda(r+\pi)\}$

(e) $\quad \dot{K} = Y\{1-\left[(1-s)+\lambda\mu+\lambda r-s\lambda\mu-s\lambda r-\lambda r-\lambda\pi\right]\}$

(f) $\quad \dot{K} = Y\{s+s\lambda\mu+s\lambda r-\lambda\mu+\lambda\pi\}$

(g) $\quad \dot{K} = Y\{s(1+\lambda\mu+\lambda r) - \lambda(\mu-\pi)\}$

(h) $\quad \dot{K} = Y\{s\left[1+\lambda(\mu+r)\right] - \lambda n\}$

(i) $\quad \dot{K} = Y\{s\left[1+\lambda(\mu-\pi+r+\pi)\right] - \lambda n\} =$

$\qquad Y\{s\left[1+\lambda(n+\pi+r)\right] - \lambda n\}$

(j) $\quad \dot{K} = F(K,L)\{s\left[1+\lambda(n+\pi+r)\right] - \lambda n\}$

Since $\dfrac{\dot{K}}{K} = n$, equation (14) can be rewritten as:

(15) $\quad \dfrac{F(K,L)}{K} \{s[1+\lambda(n+\pi+r)] - \lambda n\} = n$

Dividing the numerator and the denominator of the expression $\dfrac{F(K,L)}{K}$ by L, we have:

(16) $\quad \dfrac{\dfrac{F(K,L)}{L}}{\dfrac{K}{L}} \{s[1+\lambda(n+\pi+r)] - \lambda n\} = n$

This equation is equivalent to:

(17) $\quad \dfrac{f(k)}{k} \{s[1+\lambda(n+\pi+r)] - \lambda n\} = n$, or

(17') $\quad f(k) \{s[1+\lambda(n+\pi+r)] - \lambda n\} = nk$

Let $\sigma = \dfrac{Sp}{Y} = \{s[1+\lambda(n+\pi+r)] - \lambda n\}$. $\underline{\quad 4/}$
Equation (17') can, therefore, be reduced to the more familiar form:

(18) $\quad \sigma f(k) = nk$

Professors Levhari and Patinkin point out that $\sigma f(k)$ can be higher than $sf(k)$. Figure 12 shows that $\sigma f(k)$ can intersect the ray nk rightwards of k_1^*. This conclusion follows logically from the proposition that a monetary economy is more efficient than a barter economy. For otherwise there will be no reason for introducing money into the economy.

$\underline{4/}$ The derivation of $\sigma = \dfrac{Sp}{Y}$ is as follows:

(a) $\quad Sp = sYd - \dfrac{d}{dt}\dfrac{M}{P} = s\left[Y+\dfrac{M}{P}(\mu+r)\right] - \dfrac{M}{P}(\mu-\pi) =$

$\qquad s[Y+\lambda(\mu+r)Y] - \lambda Y(\mu-\pi)$

(b) $\quad Sp = sY[1+\lambda(\mu+r) - \lambda n] = sY[1+\lambda(n+\pi+r) - \lambda n]$

(c) $\quad \dfrac{Sp}{Y} = \sigma = s[1+\lambda(n+\pi+r) - \lambda n]$

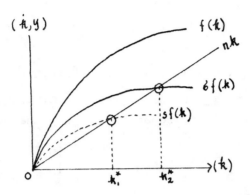

Figure 12

Money Service as a Production Good

Instead of treating them as a consumption
good, real balances can be considered as a production
good. In this case, the linearly homogeneous aggregate production function can be written as:

(19) $Y = G(K,L,\frac{M}{P})$, or, in intensive form:

(19') $y = g(k,m)$

where K may be viewed as fixed capital and M/P as
working capital.

When real balances are no longer considered
as a consumption good, disposable social income is
defined as follows:

(20) $Yd = Y + \frac{d}{dt} \frac{M}{P} = Y + \frac{M}{P}(\mu-\pi)$

It should be noted that equation (20) is different
from equation (2). The last term of equation (2),
namely, $\frac{M}{P}(r+\pi)$, is absent in equation (20). The
explanation is that money service is no longer

63

considered as a consumption good so that its imputed services are no longer included in disposable social income.

The equation for capital accumulation is now written as:

(21) $\dot{K} = G(K,L,\frac{M}{P}) - (1-s)\left[G(K,L,\frac{M}{P}) + \frac{M}{P}(\mu-\pi)\right]$

Factoring out the expression $G(K,L,\frac{M}{P})$ from the righthand side of equation (21), we have:

(22) $\dot{K} = G(K,L,\frac{M}{P})\left\{1 - (1-s)\left[1 + \dfrac{\frac{M}{P}(\mu-\pi)}{G(K,L,\frac{M}{P})}\right]\right\}$

Dividing equation (22) through by K, we obtain:

(23) $\dfrac{\dot{K}}{K} = \dfrac{G\left[K,L,\frac{M}{P}\right]}{K}\left\{1 - (1-s)\left[1 + \dfrac{\frac{M}{P}(\mu-\pi)}{G(K,L,\frac{M}{P})}\right]\right\}$

Making use of equations (11') and (12'), equation (23) is transformed into:

(24) $\dfrac{G\left[K,L,\frac{M}{P}\right]}{K}\left\{1 - (1-s)\left[1 + \dfrac{\frac{M}{P}(n)}{G(K,L,\frac{M}{P})}\right]\right\} = n$

In intensive form, equation (24) can be written as:

(25) $\dfrac{g(k,m)}{k}\left\{1 - (1-s)\left[1 + \dfrac{mn}{g(k,m)}\right]\right\} = n$

Multiplying both sides of equation (25) by k, we have:

(26) $g(k,m)\left\{1 - (1-s) - \dfrac{mn(1-s)}{g(k,m)}\right\} = nk$

Simplifying, we have:

(27) $g(k,m)\left\{s + \dfrac{(s-1)mn}{g(k,m)}\right\} = nk$

Let $\sigma^* = \dfrac{Sp}{Y} = \{s + \dfrac{(s-1)mn}{g(k,m)}\}$. Equation (27) can now be transformed into the familiar form:

(28) $\quad \sigma^* g(k,m) = nk$

The portfolio balance condition in the present case is:

(29) $\quad \dfrac{\partial g(k,m)}{\partial k} = \dfrac{\partial g(k,m)}{\partial m} - \pi$

where the expression $\dfrac{\partial g(k,m)}{\partial k}$ is the partial derivative of the production function with respect to k, the meaning of which is the own-rate of interest on physical capital; the expression $\dfrac{\partial g(k,m)}{\partial m}$ is the partial derivative of the production function with respect to m, the meaning of which is the marginal productivity of real balances per man. However, to obtain the real yield of investing in real balances, the expected rate of inflation π must be subtracted from the marginal productivity of m. This is the economic meaning of the expression on the righthand side of equation (29).

Conceivably, "per capita output in this steady state will be greater than or equal to the corresponding output in a barter economy with the same level of k: for firms in the monetary economy always have the option of carrying out production without the use of money." 5/

Comparative Dynamics

Comparative dynamics is concerned with the comparison of different steady-state growth paths that are associated with different sets of values of parameters and exogenous variables. The comparative

---

5/ Levhari and Patinkin, op. cit., p. 740.

dynamics of the two-asset neoclassical growth model
consists in examining alternative steady-state growth
paths that are associated with different target rates
of inflation π set by monetary authorities by varying
the rate of growth of the nominal money supply μ.

As a first approximation, it appears that
monetary policy can affect both the speed of adjustment and the characteristics of the steady-state growth
path. By setting a target rate of inflation through
changes in the nominal quantity of money, the monetary
authorities can change the physical savings ratio σ.
For σ depends upon λ which, in turn, depends upon k
and π. This interdependence is implied in equations
(17') and (18). More specifically, λ stands for some
fixed proportion of $\frac{M^d}{P}$ to physical output Y. In per
capita terms y = f(k). Hence λ is influenced by k.
As to the influence of π on λ, recall that a change
in π will change the opportunity costs of holding
real money balances $\left[\frac{M^d}{P}(r+\pi)\right]$. As monetary savings
decrease, physical savings rise. Thus, we can write:

(30) $\sigma = \sigma(k,\pi)$.

As σ rises, capital accumulation also increases. The economy will eventually converge to a
higher steady-state growth path with a higher k* and
y*. This hitchless convergence is illustrated by
Figure 13.

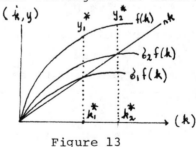

Figure 13

66

However, after careful examination, Professors Levhari and Patinkin show that it is impossible to deduce the direction of change in σ resulting from a change in π. No results hold unambiguously and all attempts to obtain comparative dynamics lead to indeterminacy. The difficulty lies in the fact that the effect of an increase in π cannot be specified a priori. For the overall savings effect is indeterminate once they give up a fixed savings ratio and assume instead a variable s as a function of r and $-\pi$. Their equation for the variable savings ratio is as follows:

(31) $s = s(r,-\pi)$.

An increase in π following an increase in μ by monetary authorities will generate a positive "composition effect." By positive "composition effect" they mean that individuals will shift away from holding real money balances towards holding physical savings. But if equation (31) holds, it is not possible to obtain unambiguous results. For, on the one hand, the increased money rate of interest following an increase in π would increase the imputed disposable income from holding real money balances (recall equation (2)); but, on the other hand, an increase in π means a decrease in the rate of return from money balances. (It will be recalled that the rate of return on money balances is $-\pi$.) Consequently, the overall savings ratio s will fall.

"A change in π will affect the steady-state value of k if and only if it affects the physical savings ratio σ. Furthermore, if the demand for money balances is [interest] inelastic, then k will change in the same direction as σ." 6/

References

Cass, D., and M. E. Yaari, "Individual Saving,
    Aggregate Capital Accumulation and Efficient
    Growth," in ESSAYS ON THE THEORY OF OPTIMAL
    GROWTH, K. Shell (Cambridge, Mass.: M.I.T.
    Press, 1967).

Johnson, H. G., ESSAYS IN MONETARY ECONOMICS
    (Cambridge, Mass.: Harvard University Press,
    1967).

Levhari, D., and D. Patinkin, "The Role of Money in
    a Simple Growth Model," American Economic
    Review, Vol. LVIII, Sept. 1968.

Marty, A. L., "The Optimal Rate of Growth of Money,"
    Journal of Political Economy," Vol. 76
    (suppl.), 1968.

Shaw, E. S., FINANCIAL DEEPENING IN ECONOMIC DEVELOP-
    MENT (New York: Oxford University Press,
    1968).

Sidrauski, M., "Inflation and Economic Growth,"
    Journal of Political Economy, Vol. LXXV,
    Dec. 1967.

_____, "Rational Choice and Patterns of Growth
    in a Monetary Economy," American Economic
    Review (suppl.), Vol. LXVII, May 1967.

Solow, R. M., GROWTH THEORY: AN EXPOSITION (New York:
    Oxford University Press, 1970).

Stein, J. L., MONEY AND CAPACITY GROWTH (New York:
    Columbia University Press, 1971).

Tobin, J., "A Dynamic Aggregative Model," Journal of
    Political Economy, Vol. LXIII, April 1955.

_____, "Money and Economic Growth," Econometrica,
    Vol. XXXIII, Oct. 1965.

_____

6/ Levhari and Patinkin, op. cit., p. 725. The word
in the bracket is inserted by us.

CHAPTER 8

A TWO-SECTOR NEOCLASSICAL GROWTH MODEL

The basic neoclassical model can be disaggregated into a two-sector growth model. With two different goods--consumption and capital goods--produced in two different sectors with different capital-intensities, other variables than those included in a one-sector model have to be taken into consideration. The additional variables involved are: (a) relative prices, (b) sectoral capital-labor ratios, (c) relative amounts of labor allotted to the two sectors, and (d) demand conditions for the output of the two sectors. Obviously, a two-sector model has to deal with a small-scale Walrasian general equilibrium problem. Consequently, the Walrasian questions of existence, uniqueness, and stability of the static and dynamic equilibrium arise.

For the sake of clarity of exposition, we shall discuss a simple two-sector neoclassical growth model in three sections. 1/ Section (A) presents a schematic table contrasting the two-sector model with the one-sector model described in Chapter 4. Section

---

1/ For more rigorous discussions of the two-sector model, see E. Burmeister and A. R. Dobell, MATHEMATICAL THEORIES OF ECONOMIC GROWTH (London, England: Macmillan, 1970) and Henry Y. Wan, Jr., ECONOMIC GROWTH (New York: Harcourt Brace Jovanovich, Inc., 1971). Also see J. E. Meade, A NEOCLASSICAL THEORY OF GROWTH (London, England: Allen & Unwin, 1961), Appendix II.

(B) explains the questions of: (a) causal determinacy
and uniqueness of static equilibrium, and (b) the
stability and uniqueness of dynamic equilibrium.
Section (C) provides an alternative graphical interpretation of the uniqueness and stability of dynamic
equilibrium developed by Professor Harry G. Johnson._2/

(A)

A SCHEMATIC TABLE SHOWING THE SIMILARITIES
AND DIFFERENCES BETWEEN THE TWO MODELS

	One-sector Model	Two-sector Model
Goods Produced	One homogeneous output a unit of which can be transformed into either one unit of a consumption good or one unit of a capital good. Hence the following metaphorical devices have been employed by writers to convey the notion: "meccano set," "ectoplasm," "putty," etc.	Two distinctly different goods are produced in two sectors of the economy--a consumption-good sector and a capital-good sector. The malleable capital good is used in the production of both goods.
Number of Assets	One durable asset only, namely, K.	One durable asset only, namely, K.
Production Functions	One aggregate linearly homogeneous production function in two inputs: capital and labor. The labor force grows at a constant exogenously	Each sector has its own linearly homogeneous pro- duction function in two inputs: capital and labor. Same assumption about the growth of labor force. An

_2/ Harry G. Johnson, THE THEORY OF INCOME DISTRIBU-
TION (London, England: Gray-Mills Publishing Ltd.,
1973), Chapter 15.

	determined proportionate rate, n; and since there is only one durable asset, an act of saving implies a corresponding demand for a capital good.	act of saving also implies a corresponding demand for a capital good.
Prices	The homogeneous output serves as the numeraire. There are no problems of changing relative prices. Thus the one-sector model excludes some important problems of capital theory, such as (a) changes in the relative prices of consumption and capital goods, and (b) the influence of changing income distribution on the steady-state growth path.	Relative prices play an essential role in the two-sector model. The model, however, emphasizes real values (not money values) in terms of a standard commodity. For convenience, the consumption good is selected as the numeraire and its price is therefore set as unity. The capital good is converted into real values in terms of the consumption good.
Mechanism for Allocating Output	The composition of the total output is uniquely determined by the overall capital-labor ratio, k; relative prices play no role in the allocation mechanism.	The production-possibilities curve is a smooth curve rather than a straight line. Therefore, the determination of the composition of the total output depends upon relative prices. The crucial variable is the factor-price ratio (wage-rental ratio) denoted by the symbol omega, ω, which in conjunction with the historically given overall capital-labor ratio, k, determines the equilibrium values of all other relevant variables of the system.

Not only output per man, but also all other relevant variables are dependent upon k.

This notion is conveyed clearly by the following equations:

(a) $y = f(k)$
(b) $r = f'(k)$
(c) $w = f(k) - kf'(k)$
(d) $S/L = sf(k)$
(e) $\dot{k} = sf(k) - nk$

Stability and Uniqueness of the Steady-state Growth Path	The uniqueness of the steady-state growth path is guaranteed by diminishing marginal product of capital. More specifically, the Inada "derivative conditions" will guarantee the existence, uniqueness, and stability of the steady-state growth path.	Diminishing marginal product of capital is not sufficient to guarantee uniqueness of the steady-state growth path. To assure stability and uniqueness of the balanced growth path, one must make an additional assumption either that the consumption-good industry is relatively more capital-intensive than the capital-good industry or that the elasticity of factor substitution in both sectors is greater than unity.
Multiple Equilibria	Multiple equilibria are ruled out by the Inada "derivative conditions." Multiple equilibria are possible only in the rare case where the savings ratio changes with the change in the capital-labor ratio.	Multiple equilibria are possible if the consumption-good industry is more labor-intensive than the capital-good industry. See the graphical interpretation in Section (C) of this chapter.

(B)

A TWO-SECTOR NEOCLASSICAL GROWTH MODEL

(I) Assumptions

(1) The following assumptions of the basic one-sector neoclassical growth model are retained:

(a) the usual static efficiency conditions of pure competition, and

(b) the exogenously determined exponential labor-force growth rate, n.

72

(2)   Additional assumptions are:

(c)   that a single malleable capital good produced by sector one is used as one of the inputs in both sectors;

(d)   that the capital-intensities of the two sectors are different;

(e)   that saving ratios from wage income and profit income are nonnegative constants denoted by s_w and s_k respectively; and

(f)   that capital depreciates at a constant exponential decay rate, δ.

(II)   <u>Causal Determinacy and Uniqueness of Static General Equilibrium</u>:

It will be recalled that for the one-sector model the growth equation can be written as a simple function $\dot{k} = \theta(k)$. <u>3/</u> For the two-sector case, the growth equation is of a more complicated form:

(1) $\dot{k} = \psi(k,x)$

where the symbol x stands for the following variables:

(a)   sectoral capital-labor ratios: k_1 and k_2, where $k = k_1 + k_2$,

(b)   labor allocation ratios: $\ell_1 = \frac{L_1}{L}$ and $\ell_2 = \frac{L_2}{L}$, where $L = L_1 + L_2$,

(c)   investment per man: $y_1 = \frac{Y_1}{L}$, where $Y = Y_1 + Y_2$,

(d)   consumption per man: $y_2 = \frac{Y_2}{L}$,

<u>3/</u> See Chapter 4 of this book. The Solovian growth equation is: $\dot{k} = sf(k) - nk$. It can be rewritten simply as: $\dot{k} = \theta(k)$. The graphical illustration of this simple equation is shown in Figure 7.

(e)   wage rate: w, and

(f)   rental rate for one unit of capital:
      $R = p_1 f_1'(k_1)$, and

(g)   aggregate savings: S. It should be noted
      that in a model without monetary assets,
      savings out of income is tantamount to
      demand for investment (capital) goods out
      of production. This is simply another
      way of stating the neoclassical proposi-
      tion that savings determine investment.

If the symbol x in equation (1) can be expressed as a function of the capital-labor ratio,
the growth equation of the two-sector model will
behave just like that of the one-sector model. This
is accomplished in the process of determining the
causality of the model.

At each instant of time the economy is depicted by an Edgeworth-Bowley box diagram the dimensions
of which are fixed by the given factor endowments.
In other words, the overall capital labor ratio, k,
is historically given at any instant of time. The
strategic variables for the solution of the static
general equilibrium problem are the historically given
k and the competitive-market determined wage-rental
ratio ($z = w/R$). Once z is found to be a function of
the capital-labor ratio, not only is it possible to
express all the relevant variables in terms of the
capital-labor ratio, but also the equilibrium condition for the output market may be stated in terms
of the same ratio.

The equilibrium wage-rental ratio is
determined as follows:

74

$$(2) \quad p_1 f_1'(k_1) = R = f_2'(k_2)$$

Equation (2) states the equilibrium condition for the capital market. The symbol p_1 stands for the price of one unit of the capital good. For convenience, the consumption good is selected as the standard commodity and its price is, therefore, set as unity, $p_2 \equiv 1$. The other prices then convert quantities into real values in terms of the consumption good. Hence, for the simple two-sector model under consideration there are three prices: (a) the price of the capital good, p_1, which is in terms of the consumption good, (b) the wage rate, w, in terms of the consumption good, and (c) the rate of profit, $r = f_1'(k_1)$, also in terms of the consumption good. Equation (2) expresses the fact that in equilibrium the rental rate of capital, R, is the same for both sectors.

$$(3) \quad p_1 f_1(k_1) - p_1 f_1'(k_1) = w =$$
$$f_2(k_2) - f_2'(k_2)k_2$$

Equation (3) depicts the equilibrium condition for the labor market. In equilibrium, the real wage rate, w, is the same everywhere.

The equilibrium wage-rental ratio is given by equation (4):

$$(4) \quad \frac{p_1 f_1(k_1) - p_1 f_1'(k_1)k_1}{p_1 f_1'(k_1)} = z =$$
$$\frac{f_2(k_2) - f_2'(k_2)k_2}{f_2'(k_2)}$$

This equation states that for any unique capital-labor ratio in each sector there corresponds a unique non-negative z.

Equation (4) may be rewritten in the following form:

$$(5) \quad z = \frac{f_i(k_i)}{f_i'(k_i)} - k_i \qquad (i = 1, 2)$$

It is obvious that $z = z(k_i)$. This relation is illustrated by Figure 14.

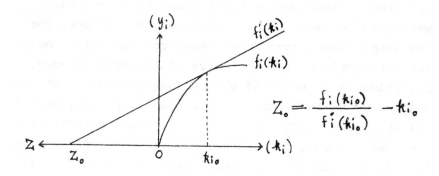

Figure 14

Since $\dfrac{dz}{dk_i} = \dfrac{-f_i(k_i) f_i''(k_i)}{\left[f_i'(k_i)\right]^2} > 0$, the function

$z = z(k_i)$ may be inverted to give:

$$(6) \quad k_i = k_i(z).$$

Thus, once the equilibrium z is determined, k_1 and k_2 are simultaneously determined by equation (6). Given k_1 and k_2, the labor allocation ratios can be expressed in terms of the capital-labor ratios as follows: 4/

$$(7) \quad \ell_1 = \frac{k_2 - k}{k_2 - k_1}$$

$$(8) \quad \ell_2 = \frac{k - k_1}{k_2 - k_1}$$

4/ The derivation of equations (7) and (8) is as follows:

(a) $K = K_1 + K_2$

Simultaneously, y_1 and y_2 are obtained in terms of the capital-labor ratio: <u>5/</u>

$$(9) \quad y_1 = \frac{I}{L} = \frac{Y_1}{L} = \ell_1 f_1(k_1) = \left[\frac{k_2 - k}{k_2 - k_1}\right] f_1(k_1)$$

$$(10) \quad y_2 = \frac{C}{L} = \frac{Y_2}{L} = \ell_2 f_2(k_2) = \left[\frac{k - k_1}{k_2 - k_1}\right] f_2(k_2)$$

Furthermore, the output market equilibrium can be obtained at the same time. The equilibrium condition for output market equilibrium is: $I = S$. However, a slight complication is introduced by the two-sector model. For the same given capital-labor ratio, k, is consistent with a multiplicity of savings ratios. This point can be made clear by looking at Figure 15 below.

$$(b) \quad K = \left(\frac{L_1}{L_1}\right) K_1 + \left(\frac{L_2}{L_2}\right) K_2 = L_1 \left(\frac{K_1}{L_1}\right) + L_2 \left(\frac{K_2}{L_2}\right) =$$

$$L_1(k_1) + L_2(k_2)$$

$$(c) \quad \frac{K}{L} = k = \frac{L_1}{L}(k_1) + \frac{L_2}{L}(k_2) = \ell_1(k_1) + \ell_2(k_2)$$

$$(d) \quad k = \ell_1(k_1) + \ell_2(k_2)$$

$$(e) \quad \ell_2 = 1 - \ell_1$$

$$(f) \quad k = \ell_1(k_1) + (1-\ell_1)(k_2) = \ell_1(k_1) + k_2 - \ell_1 k_2$$

$$(g) \quad \ell_1 = \frac{k_2 - k}{k_2 - k_1}$$

$$(h) \quad \ell_2 = 1 - \left[\frac{k_2 - k}{k_2 - k_1}\right] = \frac{k - k_1}{k_2 - k_1}$$

<u>5/</u> The derivation of equations (9) and (10) is as follows:

$$(a) \quad \frac{Y_1}{L_1} = f_1(k_1) \; ; \quad \frac{Y_2}{L_2} = f_2(k_2)$$

$$(b) \quad y_1 = \frac{Y_1}{L} = \left(\frac{L_1}{L_1}\right)\frac{Y_1}{L} = \frac{L_1}{L}\left(\frac{Y_1}{L_1}\right) = \ell_1 f_1(k_1) =$$

$$\left[\frac{k_2 - k}{k_2 - k_1}\right] f_1(k_1)$$

$$(c) \quad y_2 = \frac{Y_2}{L} = \left(\frac{L_2}{L_2}\right)\frac{Y_2}{L} = \frac{L_2}{L}\left(\frac{Y_2}{L_2}\right) = \ell_2 f_2(k_2) =$$

$$\left[\frac{k - k_1}{k_2 - k_1}\right] f_2(k_2)$$

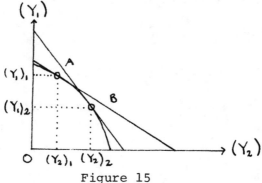

Figure 15

The production-transformation curve in Figure 15 indicates a given k, because it is derived from the contract curve in the Edgeworth-Bowley box diagram at a point in time. The same k is consistent with multiple output points such as A, B in the diagram. Since the production of investment goods corresponds to savings, the multiplicity of output points implies the multiplicity of saving ratios. Analogous to the indeterminacy of the Paretian optimum in modern welfare economics, a unique savings ratio cannot be obtained in the present case. Hence, as the Samuelson-Bergson social welfare function is introduced to obtain the unique constrained "bliss" point in welfare economics, in a similar vein, we need the Keynesian savings assumption to rule out indeterminacy in the two-sector case. For the Keynesian saving assumption makes the gross savings ratio unique and given. Thus, a unique output-market equilibrium may be obtained. A symbolic formulation of output-market equilibrium is as follows:

(11) $I = S$

(12) $P_1 Y_1 = sY = s(wL + RK)$

(13) $P_1 Y_1 = s_w(wL) + s_k(RK)$

78

(14) $\quad P_1 Y_1 = RL\left[s_w\left(\frac{W}{R}\right) + s_k\left(\frac{K}{L}\right)\right]$

(15) $\quad \frac{Y_1}{L} = \frac{R}{P_1} = f_1'(k_1)\left[s_w(z) + s_k(k)\right]$

(16) $\quad y_1 = \frac{I}{L} = \frac{S}{L} = f_1'(k_1)\left[s_w(z) + s_k(k)\right]$

Equation (11) depicts the equilibrium condition, namely, ex ante investment equals ex ante saving.
Since the value of output of sector one is the same as
gross investment in value terms, equation (12) is just
another way of stating equation (11). However, it
should be noted that the investment in equation (11)
denotes gross investment and not net investment,
because the output of sector one is used for three
separate purposes, namely, (a) net investment, $\dot{K}$,
(b) replacement investment, δK, and (c) capital widening, nK. Equation (14) is obtained by factoring out
RL from the righthand side of equation (13); equation
(15) is the outcome of dividing both sides of equation
(14) by $P_1 L$. Equation (16) is just another way of
stating equation (15).

Figure 16 illustrates the static general
equilibrium of the two-sector model.

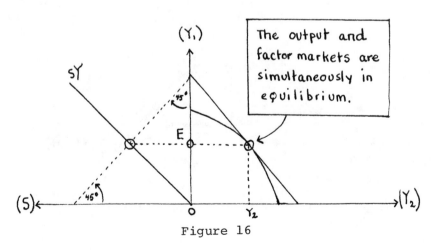

Figure 16

The diagram was originally designed by Professor
Johnson. 6/ The lefthand side of the diagram shows
the fixed savings ratio. In a one-asset model without
money or other financial assets, the supply of savings
is the same thing as the demand for investment goods
out of production. Income in terms of capital goods
is measured on the vertical axis. The 45 degree line
drawn from the vertical axis is designed to project
its intersection with the fixed savings ratio line
back to the vertical axis. Thus the point E on the
vertical axis gives the output market equilibrium condition that the demand for Y_1, or investment goods,
from savings is just equal to the supply of investment
goods out of production, which is indicated by point A
on the production transformation curve. Simultaneous
equilibrium of the factor market is depicted by the
relative price line tangent to point A. It is interesting to note that the rate of production of investment goods is not uniquely determined by the savings
ratio but also depends upon relative prices. This
point is explained by Figure 17, which is a reproduction of Figure 16 with the relative-price adjustment
processes added.

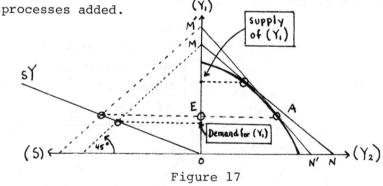

Figure 17

6/ Harry G. Johnson, op. cit., pp. 177-178.

Figure 17 shows that, if the relative-price line (factor-price ratio) is MN, the supply of investment goods out of production will be greater than the demand for them out of savings. Thus the relative-price line has to change until it is tangent to point A on the production transformation curve. The equilibrium wage-rental ratio is depicted by the line M'N'.

(III) The Stability and Uniqueness
       of Dynamic Equilibrium

After stating the causal determinacy and uniqueness of static equilibrium of the two-sector model in the preceding section, we can now proceed to derive the growth equation of the model as follows:

(16) $\frac{Y_1}{L} = \frac{S}{L} = f_1'(k_1)\left[s_w(z) + s_k(k)\right]$

(17) $Y_1 = \dot{K} + \delta K$

(18) $\dot{K} = Y_1 - \delta K$

(19) $\frac{\dot{K}}{K} = \frac{Y_1 - \delta K}{K}$

(20) $\frac{\dot{k}}{k} = \frac{\dot{K}}{K} - \frac{\dot{L}}{L} = \frac{\dot{K}}{K} - n$

(21) $\dot{k} = (\frac{\dot{K}}{K} - n)k$

(22) $\dot{k} = \left[(\frac{Y_1 - \delta K}{K}) - n\right]k$

(23) $\dot{k} = (\frac{Y_1}{K})k - \delta k - nk$

(24) $\dot{k} = (\frac{Y_1}{K})\frac{K}{L} - (\delta+n)k = \frac{Y_1}{L} - (\delta+n)k$

(25) $\dot{k} = f_1'(k_1)\left[s_w(z) + s_k(k)\right] - (\delta+n)k$

Since $z = z(k_i)$, equation (25) can be simplified as:

(26) $\dot{k} = \psi(k)$

Figure 18 is a graphical representation of equation (25).

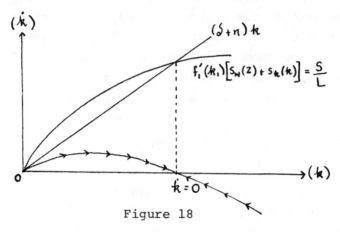

Figure 18

Equation (17) defines gross investment which is equal to net investment, $\dot{K}$, plus replacement investment, δK (where the symbol δ stands for the constant rate of depreciation). Equation (25) is the fundamental dynamic equation of the system. The "Golden Age" is attained by setting $\dot{k} = 0$, which implies $f_1'(k_1)\left[s_w(z) + s_k(k)\right] = (\delta+n)k$.

After determining the unique "golden age" growth path, we have to consider the question of stability of dynamic equilibrium. The Inada "derivative conditions" mentioned in Chapter 4 are necessary but no longer sufficient to assure dynamic stability. An additional stability condition has to be specified. Two well-known alternative stability theorems are: (a) $k_1 < k_2$, and (b) $\delta_2 \gtreqless 1$. 7/ Let us consider (a) first.

A sufficient condition to ensure the stability

7/ For a comprehensive review of the stability conditions, see E. Burmeister and A. R. Dobell, MATHEMATICAL THEORIES OF ECONOMIC GROWTH (London, England: Macmillan, 1970), pp. 120-126.

82

of dynamic equilibrium is that the capital-good
industry should be more labor-intensive than the
consumption-good industry, or $k_1 < k_2$. The significance of this stability condition may best be
illustrated by Harry Johnson's diagrammatic interpretation of the "Rybczynski theorem," 8/ which is
represented by Figure 19.

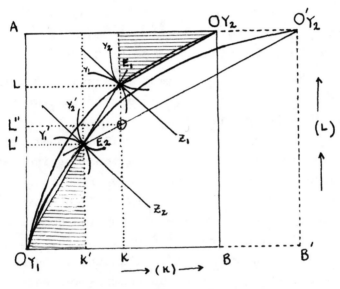

Figure 19

Figure 19 is a production-box diagram. The
initial endowment of capital is represented by AO_{Y_2}
and that of labor is AO_{Y_1}. O_{Y_1} is the origin for

8/ The original statement of the theorem comes from
T. N. Rybczynski's article, "Factor Endowment and
Relative Price," ECONOMICA, Vol. XXII, No. 4
(Nov. 1955), pp. 336-41. Harry G. Johnson's
diagram, op. cit., and MONEY, TRADE, AND ECONOMIC
GROWTH (Cambridge, Mass.: Harvard University Press,
1967), pp. 87-89.

sector one and O_{Y_2} the origin for sector two. $O_{Y_2}O_{Y_1}$ is the contract curve. Suppose that the point E_1 is the pre-capital-growth production point. The slope of the ray $O_{Y_1}E_1$ measures k_1 and that of the ray $O_{Y_2}E_1$ measures k_2. It is obvious that $k_1 < k_2$. At point E_1 the economy produces Y_2 consumption goods (indicated by the isoquant Y_2) and Y_1 capital goods (indicated by the isoquant Y_1). The production of Y_2 employs AL of labor and BK of capital. The production of Y_1 uses $O_{Y_1}L$ of labor and $O_{Y_1}K$ of capital. The equilibrium wage-rental ratio is given by the slope of the common tangent to the two isoquants at point E_1.

The "Rybczynski theorem," in essence, states that: (a) if the production functions of the two sectors are linearly homogeneous, and (b) if the MRTS in production of the two sectors, as well as the factor-price ratio, remain unchanged, an autonomous increase in one factor, say capital, would give rise to an expansion in the production of the capital-intensive good (in the present case, the consumption-good industry) and a reduction in the production of the labor-intensive good. This theorem is illustrated by Figure 19. Suppose that there is an autonomous increase in capital from O_{Y_2} to O'_{Y_2}. Thus the origin of sector-two is shifted from O_{Y_2} to O'_{Y_2}. Consequently the contract curve is altered to $O_{Y_1}O'_{Y_2}$. The constant capital-labor ratios are indicated by the original ray $O_{Y_1}E_1$ and the ray $O'_{Y_2}E_2$ which is parallel to $O_{Y_2}E_1$. The constant relative prices (and hence the wage-rental ratio) is depicted by the common tangent to the isoquants Y'_1 and Y'_2 at E_2, which is parallel to that at E_1.

It should be noted that the production of capital goods at E_2 is lower than that at E_1. This reduction is necessary to maintain stability of equilibrium. For the reduction of the labor-intensive good will release just the right extra amount of labor required to operate the additional capital. In Figure 19 the amount of labor released by sector one is measured by the distance LL' and the amount of capital released by the same sector is measured by the distance KK'. However, only L'L" of labor released is required to operate KK', leaving LL" free to operate the new capital BB' ($= O_{Y_2} O'_{Y_2}$). Thus a unique equilibrium is again attained.

The "Rybczynski theorem" is illustrated alternatively by Figure 20. The autonomous capital accumulation is depicted by the outward shift of the production-transformation curve. The original equilibrium position is E_1 which corresponds to E_1 of Figure 19; the new equilibrium position is E_2 which corresponds to E_2 of Figure 19. The constant wage-rental ratio is represented by the parallel relative-price lines tangent to E_1 and E_2 (corresponding to Z_1 and Z_2 of Figure 19).

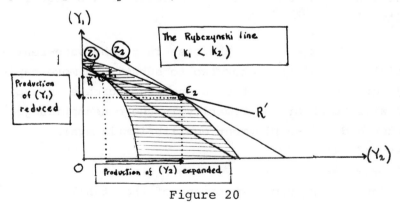

Figure 20

The downward-sloping RR' is the Rybczynski line, which reflects the stability condition $k_1 < k_2$. If the assumption is reversed, i.e., $k_1 > k_2$, the Rybczynski line will have a positive slope. Putting it differently, the Rybczynski line is the locus of the points on successive production-transformation curves for which the commodity price ratio and hence the factor price ratio are constant. It is only a reference line designed by Harry Johnson to be used in the derivations of the investment requirements curve and investment supply curve which will be discussed in the following Section (C).

Turning now to the stability condition (b), namely, the elasticity of substitution of sector two should be greater or equal to unity, $\delta \gtreqless 1$, the economic interpretation of this alternative stability condition is as follows:

Suppose that the economy is initially in steady-state growth equilibrium. Then an autonomous increase in capital occurs (such as foreign aid). This disturbance will force both the wage-rental ratio and the capital-labor ratios to rise and the marginal product of capital to fall. If the elasticity of factor substitution of sector two is greater than or equal to unity, $\delta_2 = \dfrac{\frac{dk_2}{k_2}}{\frac{dz}{z}} \gtreqless 1$, the rise in z (the wage-rental ratio) will induce sector two to substitute more capital for labor. Thus, the autonomous increase in capital will be absorbed primarily in the consumption-good sector and full-employment equilibrium is again restored. 9/

9/ For more rigorous statement of the stability

(C)

THE JOHNSONIAN GRAPHICAL INTERPRETATION OF
THE STABILITY AND UNIQUENESS OF THE
STEADY-STATE GROWTH PATH <u>10</u>/

The objective of the following diagrams is to
bring together the essential points considered in the
preceding Section (B). The two principal geometrical
devices are the investment requirements curve denoted
by the symbol Ir and the investment supply curve represented by the symbol Is. The Ir curve is derived
from the Rybczynski line and the investment requirements line, both of which are reference lines. The
former reflects the stability condition, $k_1 < k_2$; the
latter is the analog of the "golden-age" line in
Figure 18. The Rybczynski line has been explained in
the preceding section. The graphical explanation of
the investment requirements line is given by Figure 21
which consists of two panels.

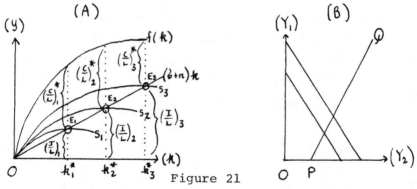

Figure 21

---

conditions, see E. M. Drandakis, "Factor Sub-
stitutions in the Two-Sector Growth Model,"
REVIEW OF ECONOMIC STUDIES, 1963, pp. 217-28.

<u>10</u>/ Harry G. Johnson, THE THEORY OF INCOME DIS-
TRIBUTION, Chapter 15.

Panel (A) is simply a reproduction of the diagram for the one-sector neoclassical growth model. Since the two-sector model can be reduced to $\dot{k} = \psi(k)$ which is similar to the growth equation of the one-sector model, therefore, for the sake of simplicity, we use the diagram in Panel (A) to illustrate some essential points. The "golden-age" line in Panel (A) is indicated by the $(\delta+n)k$ line, which is a locus of points describing the amount of investment per man $(\frac{I}{L})$ required to maintain the constancy of the capital-labor ratio (k*) at successively higher (k*'s). The investment requirements line of Professor Johnson is the line PQ of Panel (B), which is analogous to the $(\delta+n)k$ line of Panel (A). For it is also a locus of points depicting the required investment to maintain the constancy of the capital-labor ratio at successively higher k represented by successively higher but parallel factor-price lines. In other words, it is the locus of points analogous to E_1, E_2, E_3, and so on depicted by Panel (A). It is obvious that both the $(\delta+n)k$ line and the investment requirements line PQ are reference lines similar to the 45 degree line of the Keynesian cross diagram.

Figure 22 is the diagram for the investment requirements curve, Ir, which is the locus of points describing the required investment to sustain the long-run consumption possibilities open to the economy. It is not the same as the investment requirements line PQ. Whereas PQ is analogous to the $(\delta+n)k$ line in Panel (A) of Figure 21, Ir depicts the $(\frac{I}{L})_1$, $(\frac{I}{L})_2$, $(\frac{I}{L})_3$, . . . necessary to sustain the corresponding $(\frac{C}{L})_1^*$, $(\frac{C}{L})_2^*$, $(\frac{C}{L})_3^*$, . . . pictured in the same panel. The derivation of the Ir curve is as follows: Projecting the

88

amount of capital-good production shown on PQ back to
the corresponding production-transformation curve, we
obtain one point on the Ir curve. By repeating the
process, the Ir curve is derived. It should be noted
that the Ir curve will be tangent to PQ at only one
point--where the latter intersects the RR' line. The
point at which the Ir curve starts to bend back on
itself towards the vertical axis is the "golden-rule"
point.

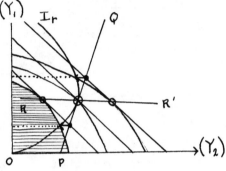

Figure 22

It should also be noted that the Ir curve is independent of any assumption about the capital-labor ratios
of the two sectors.

Figure 23 shows the derivation of the investment supply curve, Is, which is the locus of points at
which the demand for investment goods out of savings
just matches the supply of investment goods out of
production. This equality is depicted by the point E
in Figure 23. When autonomous capital accumulation
occurs, the production-transformation curve shifts
outwards. If the factor-price ratio remains unchanged
as indicated by the line Z_2, which is parallel to the
initial Z_1, the production point will move along the
Rybczynski line to the point B. However, at this

89

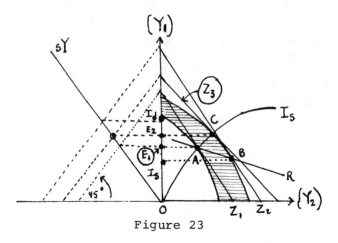

Figure 23

point the supply of investment goods denoted by Is on
the vertical axis will be insufficient to meet the
demand for investment goods out of savings as indicated by the point Id on the vertical axis. Consequently, the price of capital goods will rise. The
relative price adjustment will lead to the new equilibrium position at point C. Once again the demand
for and the supply of capital goods are made equal.
This equality is depicted by point E_2 on the vertical
axis. In the case of $k_1 < k_2$, the Is curve is concave
to the horizontal axis. If the capital-labor assumption is reversed $(k_1 > k_2)$, Is will be concave to the
vertical axis. Unlike the Ir curve, the investment
supply curve is dependent on the capital-labor ratio
assumptions.

Putting the Ir and Is curve into juxtaposition,
we obtain the graphical representation of the stable
and unique steady-state growth path, which is illustrated by Figure 24.

90

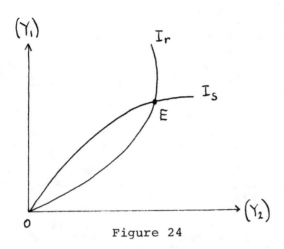

Figure 24

If the capital-good production is more capital-intensive than that of the consumption good ($k_1 > k_2$), the long-run growth equilibrium may either be stable and unique, or have multiple equilibria. These possibilities are illustrated by Panel (A) and Panel (B) of Figure 25.

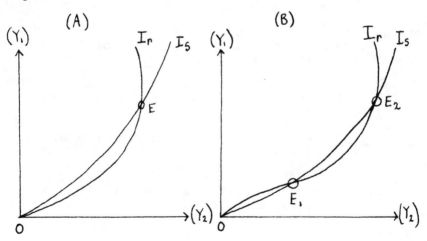

Figure 25

References

Burmeister, E., and A. R. Dobell, MATHEMATICAL THEORIES OF ECONOMIC GROWTH (London, England: Macmillan, 1970).

Drandakis, E. M., "Factor Substitution in the Two-Sector Growth Model," Review of Economic Studies, Vol. XXX, Oct. 1963.

Inada, K., "On a Two-Sector Model of Economic Growth: Comments and a Generalization," Review of Economic Studies, Vol. XXX, June 1963.

_____, "On the Stability of Growth Equilibria in Two-Sector Models," Review of Economic Studies, Vol. XXXI, April 1964.

Johnson, H. G., MONEY, TRADE, AND ECONOMIC GROWTH (Cambridge, Mass.: Harvard University Press, 1967).

_____, THE THEORY OF INCOME DISTRIBUTION (London, England: Gray-Mills Publishing Ltd., 1973).

Meade, J. E., A NEOCLASSICAL THEORY OF GROWTH (London, England: Allen & Unwin, 1961).

Rybczynski, T. N., "Factor Endowments and Relative Price," Economica, Vol. XXII, No. 4, Nov. 1955.

Solow, R. M., "Note on Uzawa's Two-Sector Model of Economic Growth," Review of Economic Studies, Vol. XXIX, Oct. 1961.

Uzawa, H., "On a Two-Sector Model of Economic Growth I," Review of Economic Studies, Vol. XXIX, Oct. 1961.

_____, "On a Two-Sector Model of Economic Growth II," Review of Economic Studies, Vol. XXX, June 1963.

Wan, H. Y., ECONOMIC GROWTH (New York: Harcourt Brace Jovanovich, Inc., 1971).

Chapter 9

OPTIMAL NEOCLASSICAL GROWTH MODEL

The optimal neoclassical growth model considered
in this chapter is part of dynamic normative economics.
It involves the choosing of the optimal time paths of
some strategic variables, which will best satisfy some
social objective. Hence, it is essentially a planning
problem. As such, the neoclassical model is no longer
objectionable to its critics. For it is well known
that the theory of perfectly-competitive capitalism is
equivalent in many respects to the theory of a planned
or socialist economy.[1] Professor Joan Robinson observes:

> However, there is one point on which I agree
> with him (Professor Solow) - that the notion
> of factor allocation in conditions of per-
> fect competition makes sense in a normative
> theory for a planned economy rather than in
> a descriptive theory for a capitalist econ-
> omy, and that the notion of marginal pro-
> ductivity of investment makes sense in the
> context of socialist planning.[2]

The model's dynamic normative qualifications can
be further clarified by an analogy between welfare
economics and optimal neoclassical growth theory.
For optimal neoclassical growth theory can be viewed as
dynamic welfare economics. However, as Professor John
Hicks puts it, this aspect of dynamic welfare economics
faces all the standard difficulties of static welfare

---

[1]See O. Lange and F. Taylor, On the Economic Theory of
Socialism (University of Minnesota Press, 1938) and E.
Barone, "The Ministry of Production in the Collectiv-
ist State," in F.A. Hayek (ed.), Collectivist Economic
Planning (Routledge & Kegan Paul, 1935), pp. 247-90.

[2]Joan Robinson, "Solow on the Rate of Return," in Col-
lected Economic Papers, Vol. 3 (Blackwell, 1965), pp.
36-47. Reprinted in G.C. Harcourt and N.F. Laing, eds.,
Capital and Growth, Penguin Modern Economics Readings
(Middlesex, England: Penguin Books, Ltd., 1971), p. 168.
The words in the brackets are ours.

economics, such as (a) interpersonal comparisons, (b) the problem of increasing returns, (c) external economies and diseconomies, and so on. Thus, "the lions in the path of static theory - all remain with us. It it just as intractable as static theory."[3] With these characteristics of the model sketched as background, we will proceed to elucidate its methodology.

The optimal neoclassical growth theory is an optimal control problem. Generally speaking, there are three different but related approaches to solving the optimal control problem, namely, by: (a) calculus of variations, (b) dynamic programming, and (c) Pontryagin's maximum principle.[4] Professor Robert Dorfman describes the contribution to economics from the use of these approaches:

> In its modern version, the calculus of variations is called optimal control theory. It has become, deservedly, the central tool of capital theory and has given the latter a new lease on life. As a result, capital theory has become so profoundly transformed that it has been rechristened growth theory, and has come to grips with numerous important practical and theoretical issues that previously could not even be formulated.[5]

In this chapter we limit ourselves to the application of the Pontryagin maximum principle to a simple optimal neoclassical growth model.[6] The maximum principle may be regarded as an extension of the method of

[3] John Hicks, Capital and Growth (New York: Oxford University Press, 1965), pp. 201-202.

[4] For comprehensive explanations see Michael D. Intriligator, Mathematical Optimization and Economic Theory (Englewood Cliffs, N.J.: Prentice-Hall, 1971), Chapter 12; G. Hadley and M.C. Kemp, Variational Methods in Economics (New York: American Elsevier Publishing Co., Inc., 1971), Chapter 4; and Akira Takayama, Mathematical Economics (Hinsdale, Ill.: The Dryden Press, 1974), Chapter 5.

[5] Robert Dorfman, "An Economic Interpretation of Optimal Control Theory," American Economic Review, Vol. LIX, No. 5, p. 817.

[6] L.S. Pontryagin, V.G. Boltyanskii, R.V. Gamkrelidze, and

Lagrange multipliers used in static, constrained optimization theory to one applicable to dynamic, constrained
optimization problems. From elementary microeconomics,
we are familiar with the Lagrange multiplier method in
maximizing consumer utility and in finding the firm's
least-cost combination of inputs. The similarities
and differences between the static Lagrange multiplier
method and the Pontryagin maximum principle may be
brought out in sharp relief by means of the following
schematic table on pages 96 and 97.

The left-hand side of the schematic table shows
the familiar constrained optimization problem of the
consumer in elementary microeconomics. The objective
function to be maximized is the utility function,
$U = U(X, Y)$, where the two commodities, X and Y, are
the choice variables. The budget constraint is the
equation

$$P_{X_c} X + P_{Y_c} Y - I_c = 0$$

where P_{X_c} and P_{Y_c} are the given prices of the two commodities and I_c is the given budget. With a view to trans-
forming the constrained-maximization problem into a
free-extremum one, an augmented objective function is
constructed in the form of

$$Z(x, y, \lambda) = U + \lambda\left[P_{x_o} x + P_{y_o} y - I_o\right]$$

where λ is the Lagrange multiplier, which is to be
treated as an extra variable. As the first-order condition, we have the following set of simultaneous
equations:

$$\left. \begin{array}{l} \dfrac{\partial Z}{\partial x} = \dfrac{\partial U}{\partial x} - \lambda P_{x_o} = 0 \\[2mm] \dfrac{\partial Z}{\partial y} = \dfrac{\partial U}{\partial y} - \lambda P_{y_o} = 0 \end{array} \right\} \quad \dfrac{\frac{\partial U}{\partial x}}{P_{x_o}} = \dfrac{\frac{\partial U}{\partial y}}{P_{y_o}} = \lambda$$

$$\dfrac{\partial Z}{\partial \lambda} = P_{x_o} x + P_{y_o} y - I_o = 0$$

Figure 26 illustrates the constrained-optimization
problem of the consumer.

E.F. Mishchenko, The Mathematical Theory of Optimal
Process (translated by K.N. Trirogoff) (New York:
Interscience Publishers, John Wiley & Sons, Inc., 1962);
and E. Burmeister and A.R. Dobell, op. cit., Chapter 11.

A Schematic Table Showing the Similarities and Differences Between the Static Lagrange Multiplier and the Pontryagin Maximum Principle

STATIC LAGRANGE MULTIPLIER	DYNAMIC LAGRANGE MULTIPLIER (MAXIMUM PRINCIPLE)
Objection Function: $$U = U(X,Y)$$ Constraint: $$P_{X_0} X + P_{Y_0} Y - I_0 = 0$$	Objective Functional: $$\max W = \int_{t_0}^{T} U(c)\, dt = \int_{t_0}^{T} U\left[f(k) - nk - \dot{k}\right] dt$$ Constraints: (a) Transversality Conditions: $$k(t_0) = k_0 \; ; \; k(T) = k_T$$ (b) The transition equation: $$\dot{k} = f(k) - nk - c$$
The Augmented Objective Function: (the Lagrangian Expression) $$Z(X,Y,\lambda) = U + \lambda\left[P_{X_0} + P_{Y_0} - I_0\right]$$	The Hamiltonian Equation (the Lagrangian Expression): $$H = U(c) + \lambda(\dot{k})$$
The Static Lagrange Multiplier: $$\lambda$$	The Dynamic Lagrange Multiplier: $$\lambda$$
Constrained Static Optimization: $$\frac{\partial Z}{\partial X} = \frac{\partial U}{\partial X} - \lambda P_{X_0} = 0$$ $$\frac{\partial Z}{\partial Y} = \frac{\partial U}{\partial Y} - \lambda P_{Y_0} = 0$$ $$\frac{\partial Z}{\partial \lambda} = P_{X_0} X + P_{Y_0} Y - I_0 = 0$$ $$\frac{\dfrac{\partial U}{\partial X}}{P_{X_0}} = \frac{\dfrac{\partial U}{\partial Y}}{P_{Y_0}} = \lambda$$	Constrained Dynamic Optimization: For an optimum, it is necessary that the Hamiltonian be constant over time. The necessary and sufficient conditions for $H = 0$ are as follows: (c) $\frac{\partial H}{\partial c} = 0$, implying $\lambda = U'(c)$ (d) $\frac{\partial H}{\partial \lambda} = \dot{k}$ (e) $-\frac{\partial H}{\partial k} = \dot{\lambda}$, implying $\dot{\lambda} = -\lambda\left[f'(k) - n\right]$ These conditions imply that the three optimal time paths for the control variable (c), the state variable (k), and the co-state variable (λ) will attain steady-state equilibrium growth.

$$\text{(f)} \quad \dot{c} = \frac{c}{\delta}\left[f'(k) - n\right] = 0$$

$$\text{(g)} \quad \dot{k} = f(k) - nk - c = 0$$

$$\text{(h)} \quad \dot{\lambda} = -\lambda\left[f'(k) - n\right] = 0$$

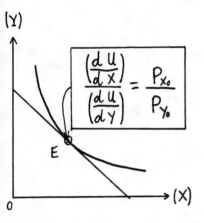

Figure 26

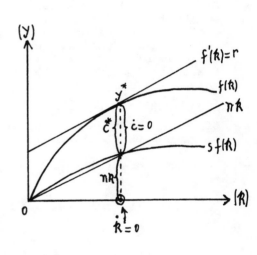

Figure 27

97

The right-hand side of the schematic table shows the application of the maximum principle to an optimal neoclassical growth model. Before explaining the meaning of the objective functional, let us first state the optimal control problem involved in the present case. Suppose the economic objective of a central planning board is to raise the standard of living of the people, as measured by consumption per man,

$$c \equiv \frac{C}{L} .$$

Further, assume that the planning board has a utility function expressing utility as a function of consumption per man:

(1) $U = U(c)$, $U'(c) > 0$, $U''(c) < 0$.

Then, the dynamic economizing problem confronting the planning board is that of choosing the optimal time paths for c over the relevant planning period from t_o to the terminal time, T, so as to maximize the welfare derived from the optimum time path or trajectory for c. Here lies the difference between the two problems. In the case of static optimization, the problem is to choose the optimal values of the two choice (independent) variables, X and Y, that maximize the value of the objective function U. The dynamic optimization problem, on the other hand, is to choose the optimal time path (instead of values) of the control variable c from a given class of time paths, called the control set.

The constraints of the optimal neoclassical growth model are:

(a)   The transversality conditions: $k(t_o) = k_o$;

k(T) = k_T, where k is called the state variable. k_o denotes the capital-labor ratio at the initial state; and k_T stands for the capital-labor ratio at the terminal planning period. The relevant interval is assumed given and the terminal time can be finite or infinite.

(b)   The time path of capital accumulation, given the equation:

$\dot{k} = f(k) - nk - c.$[7] The explanation is simply that the linearly homogeneous aggregate production function in per capita terms is $y = f(k)$. It is clear that y depends upon k. Since y is also equal to the sum of consumption per man, c, net investment per man, $\dot{k}$, and investment per man required for capital-widening, nk, or $f(k) = c + \dot{k} + nk$, it follows that the time path for c cannot be independent of the time path for k.

Turning now to the dynamic optimization problem, the objective functional is written as:

$$(2) \quad \max W = \int_{t_0}^{T} U(c)\,dt = \int_{t_0}^{T} F\,dt = \int_{t_0}^{T} U\left[f(k) - nk - \dot{k}\right] dt$$

where W denotes the social welfare function to be maximized. W is obtained by integrating all instantaneous contributions to utility by consumption per man over the relevant planning period. F is sometimes referred to as the performance curve. It is the same as U $[f(k) - nk - \dot{k}]$. This expression is obtained simply by substituting the equation $c = f(k) - nk - \dot{k}$ into equation (1). The concepts of the performance curve and the maximization of the objective functional are depicted by Figure 28.

Figure 28

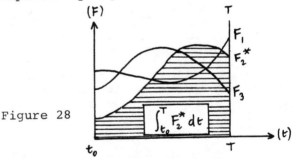

---

[7]The equation is derived from the identity equation: $f(k) = c + \dot{k} + nk.$ $\dot{k} = f(k) - nk - c$, and $c = f(k) - nk - \dot{k}.$

The optimal performance curve is F_2^* and the shaded area under F_2^* is the maximand. The other feasible trajectories are indicated by F_1 and F_3 in the control set.

The analog of the augmented objective function of the static optimization problem is the Hamiltonian equation, which is a Lagrangian expression. The Hamiltonian is written as:

$$(3) \quad H = U(c) + \lambda \, (\dot{k})$$

This is a Legendre transformation of equation (2) into an equivalent form, after introducing a new variable, λ, the dynamic Lagrange multiplier, which is defined as

$$(4) \quad \lambda = U'(c) = U'(f(k) - nk - \dot{k}).$$

The transformation also requires that we solve the system to obtain $\dot{k}$ as a function of k, λ, and t.

It should be noted that the Hamiltonian is the sum of three elements: (1) the integrand of the objective functional $U(c)$; (2) the costate variable (the dynamic Lagrange multiplier) λ; and (3) the constraint $\dot{k}$. Furthermore, the Hamiltonian may be considered as total output measured in terms of per capita utility $U(c)$. This is because the two components of total output are: (1) the utility of the consumption flow, namely $U(c)$ and (2) the marginal utility derived from additional capital per man $\lambda \, (\dot{k})$, where λ can be viewed as the marginal utility of per-capita consumption $U'(c)$, or "shadow price" of capital accumulation. This point will be clarified in the following paragraph. At this juncture, one may recall the well-known theorem in linear programming theory that the Lagrange multipliers in the Primal problem turn out to be the "shadow prices" in the Dual problem.[8]

To achieve an optimal policy, i.e., to maximize the Hamiltonian over time, three specific requirements should

---

[8] See William J. Baumol, Economic Theory and Operations Analysis (Englewood Cliffs, N.J.: Prentice-Hall, 1977), 4th edition, Chapter 6.

be satisfied. As a first order condition, H is maximized by the choice of $\dot{k}$.

(5) $\quad \dfrac{\partial H}{\partial \dot{k}} = \dfrac{\partial U(c)}{\partial \dot{k}} + \lambda = 0$

which yields

(6) $\quad \lambda = U'(c)$

which is exactly the same as equation (4). The two other conditions for achieving an optimal policy are the following canonical equations for the costate variable λ:

(a) $\quad \dfrac{\partial H}{\partial \lambda} = \dot{k}$

(b) $\quad -\dfrac{\partial H}{\partial k} = \dot{\lambda}$, implying

$$\dot{\lambda} = -\lambda[f'(k) - n].$$

The derivation of equation (a) is as follows:

(7) $\quad \dfrac{\partial}{\partial \lambda} = \dfrac{\partial}{\partial \lambda} U(c) + \dfrac{\partial}{\partial \lambda}\lambda\dot{k} = U'\left(\dfrac{-\partial \dot{k}}{\partial \lambda}\right) + \dot{k} + \lambda\dfrac{\partial \dot{k}}{\partial \lambda}$

From (6), $U' = \lambda$; substituting this into (7) we get

(8) $\quad \dfrac{\partial H}{\partial \lambda} = \lambda\left(\dfrac{-\partial \dot{k}}{\partial \lambda}\right) + \dot{k} + \lambda\dfrac{\partial \dot{k}}{\partial \lambda} + \lambda\dfrac{\partial \dot{k}}{\partial \lambda} = \dot{k}.$

The derivation of equation (b) is as follows:

(9) $\quad \dfrac{\partial H}{\partial k} = \dfrac{\partial}{\partial k}U(f(k) - nk - \dot{k}) + \dfrac{\partial}{\partial k} \lambda\dot{k} =$

$$U'[f'(k) - n] - U'\dfrac{\partial \dot{k}}{\partial k} + \lambda\dfrac{\partial \dot{k}}{\partial k}$$

Since $U' = \lambda$, then

(10) $\quad \dfrac{\partial H}{\partial k} = U'[f'(k) - n].$

To show the relationship between $\dfrac{\partial H}{\partial k}$ and $\dot{\lambda}$ we differentiate equation (6) with respect to time:

(11) $\dfrac{d\lambda}{dt} = U''\left[f'(k)\dfrac{dk}{dt} - n\dfrac{dk}{dt} - \dfrac{\dot{dk}}{dt}\right]$ or

(12) $\dot{\lambda} = U''[f'(k)\dot{k} - n\dot{k} - \ddot{k}] = \dot{U}'$

Now, along an optimal accumulation path, the Euler-Lagrange equation should be satisfied; i.e.,

(13) $\dfrac{\partial U(c)}{\partial k} = \dfrac{d}{dt} \cdot \dfrac{\partial U(c)}{\partial \dot{k}}$ or

(14) $U'[f'(k) - n] = -\dot{U}'$

Substituting (14) into (12) we obtain

(15) $\dot{\lambda} = -U'[f'(k) - n]$

From (15) and (10) we get

(16) $\dot{\lambda} = -\dfrac{\partial H}{\partial k}$

And, substituting for $U' = \lambda$ in (15) we get

(17) $\dot{\lambda} = -\lambda[f'(k) - n].$

In summary, an optimal policy can now be presented by the following three equations:

(18) $\bar{H} = U[f(k) - nk - \dot{k}(k, \lambda, t)] + \lambda \dot{k}(k, \lambda, t)$

(19) $\dot{k} = \dfrac{\partial \bar{H}}{\partial \lambda}$

(20) $\dot{\lambda} = -\dfrac{\partial \bar{H}}{\partial k} = -U'[f'(k) - n].$

They guarantee that the Hamiltonian will be maximized. The proof is as follows:

(21) $\dot{H} = \dfrac{dH}{dt} = U'(c)\dot{c} + \lambda\ddot{k} + \dot{k}\dot{\lambda}$

(22) $\lambda = u'(c)$

(23) $\dot{\lambda} = -\lambda[f'(k) - n]$

Substituting (5) and (6) into (4) yields:

$$(24) \quad \dot{H} = \lambda \, \dot{c} + \lambda \, \ddot{k} + \dot{k} \left\{ -\lambda [f'(k) - n] \right\}$$

Rearranging terms one has:

$$(25) \quad \dot{H} = \lambda \, \dot{c} + \lambda \, \ddot{k} - \lambda \, \dot{k} f'(k) + \lambda \, n\dot{k} =$$
$$\lambda \, [\dot{c} + \ddot{k} - \dot{k} f'(k) + n\dot{k}].$$

$$(26) \quad \frac{dk}{dt} = \ddot{k} = \frac{d}{dt} [f(k) - nk - c] = f'(k)\dot{k} - n\dot{k} - \dot{c}.$$

Rearranging terms yields:

$$(27) \quad \dot{c} + \ddot{k} = \dot{k} f'(k) - n\dot{k}$$

Substituting (27) into (25), one obtains:

$$(28) \quad \dot{H} = \lambda \left[\dot{k} f'(k) - n\dot{k} - \dot{k} f'(k) + n\dot{k} \right] = 0.$$

We now have two time paths: one for the state variable which is

$$\dot{k} = f(k) - nk - c;$$

the other for the costate variable, namely, $\dot{\lambda} = -\lambda [f'(k)-n]$, which may be rewritten as:

$$(29) \quad \frac{\dot{\lambda}}{\lambda} = -[f'(k) - n] \quad \text{or} \quad (29') \quad f'(k) + \frac{\dot{\lambda}}{\lambda} - n = 0.$$

The economic meaning of equation (29') is that the net profit of holding a unit of k is equal to zero. For f'(k) stands for the marginal product of capital or internal rate of return to capital in per capita terms; $\frac{\dot{\lambda}}{\lambda}$ denotes capital gains (because λ is the imputed value of additional k); and n indicates the dilution of equity through population growth. Net profit = $f'(k) + \frac{\dot{\lambda}}{\lambda} - n$. In the present case, it is equal to zero. This is a long-run equilibrium condition for a competitive economy.

The solution for the optimal neoclassical growth model, however, requires a third time path, namely the time path of the control variable c. The derivation of the time path for c is as follows:

(30) $\dot{\lambda} = \dfrac{d\lambda}{dt} = \dfrac{d}{dt}\ U'(c) = U''(c).\dot{c}$

Dividing equation (30) by λ yields

(31) $\dfrac{\dot{\lambda}}{\lambda} = \dfrac{U''(c)}{\lambda} \cdot \dot{c} = \dfrac{U''(c)}{U'(c)} \cdot \dot{c}$

To eliminate the expression $\dfrac{U''(c)}{U'(c)}$, we introduce the equation for the elasticity of marginal utility with respect to per capita consumption:

(32) $\mathcal{C} = -\dfrac{\dfrac{du'}{u'}}{\dfrac{dc}{c}} = -\dfrac{du'}{u'} \cdot \dfrac{c}{dc} = -\dfrac{du'}{dc} \cdot \dfrac{c}{u'} = -U''(c)\dfrac{c}{u'(c)}$

Rearranging terms, one obtains:

(33) $-\dfrac{\mathcal{C}}{c} = \dfrac{u''(c)}{u'(c)}$

Substituting equations (29) and (33) into equation (31) yields:

(34) $-[f'(k) - n] = -\dfrac{\mathcal{C}}{c} \cdot \dot{c}$

Rearranging terms, we finally obtain the equation for the time path of c:

(35) $\dot{c} = \dfrac{c}{\mathcal{C}} [f'(k) - n].$

Optimal growth requires $\dot{c} = 0$. In this case, equation (35) collapses into the "Golden Rule of Accumulation":[9]

(36) $f'(k^*) = n$

where k* denotes the optimal capital-labor ratio.

---

[9] See E.S. Phelps, _Golden Rules of Economic Growth_ (New York: Norton, 1966). The "Golden Rule" may be stated simply as follows: (1) The components of "golden age" output per man, y*, are: y* = f(k*) = c* + nk*. (2) Therefore, C* = f(k*) - nk*. (3) Choosing the optimal k* to maximize c* means differentiating equation (2) with respect to k* and setting it equal to zero. Thus, we have: dc*/dk* = f'(k*) - n = 0. Rearranging terms yields: (4) f'(k*) = n.

Optimal growth also requires $\dot{k} = 0$. If so, the equation for the time path of k, namely,

$$\dot{k} = f(k) - nk - c,$$

is transformed into the following equation:

(37) $f(k^*) = nk^* + c^*.$

If equation (36) holds, equation (29) gives us another optimal condition, namely,

$$\dot{\lambda} = 0.$$

Figure 29 (which is a reproduction of Figure 27 included in the schematic table) illustrates the optimal conditions depicted by equations (36) and (37).

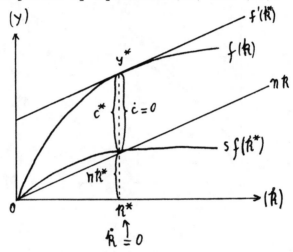

Figure 29

Economic growth, however, cannot be obtained without costs. The alternative cost of increasing the growth rate is the current consumption foregone. The central planning board may have a high rate of time preference, favoring the near future utilities derived from per capita consumption over the more distant ones. In this case, a constant exponential discount rate $e^{-\psi}$ may be

introduced into the model; and optimal growth would then follow a modified "Golden Rule" path. The objective functional is then written as:

105

(38) $\max\ W = \int_{t_0}^{T} e^{-\psi} U(c)\,dt$

The Hamiltonian is modified as:

(39) $H(c, k, \lambda) = e^{-\psi}\left\{U(c) + \lambda(\dot{k})\right\}$

Consequently, the modified "Golden Rule" condition is:

(40) $f'(k^*) = n + \psi$

Figure 30 illustrates the modified "Golden Rule" growth path.

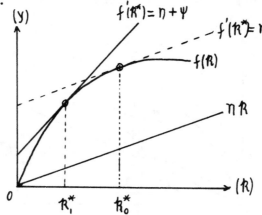

Figure 30

The lower growth rate reflects the intention of the central planning board to seek an optimum rather than a maximum rate of growth that would achieve the best balance between the gains from growth to future generations and the losses in per capita consumption to the current generation.

The structure of the solution can be alternatively described by a phase diagram in the (c, k) plane.

Figure 31 consists of three panels. Panel (A) is the phase diagram for the two differential equations:

$\dot{c} = \frac{c}{\sigma}[f'(k) - n]$ and $\dot{k} = f(k) - nk - c.$

106

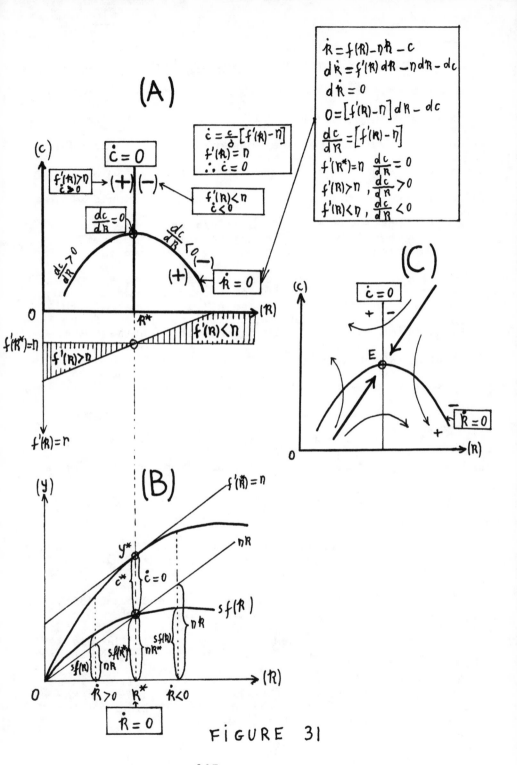

FIGURE 31

The vertical axis measures c and the horizontal axis measures k. The two isokines are $\dot{c}$ = 0 and $\dot{k}$ = 0. Isokines are equal-movement curves. The isokine for $\dot{c}$ = 0 shows the various combinations of c's and k's for which $\dot{c}$ would be equal to zero; and the isokine $\dot{k}$ = 0 similarly describes the combinations of c and k that would yield $\dot{k}$ = 0. The lower part of panel (A) shows the relationship between f'(k) and k. The negative slope reflects the diminishing marginal productivity of capital.

Focusing attention first on the isokine $\dot{k}$ = 0, one sees that the general shape of the isokine depends upon the relation between f'(k) and n. To demonstrate this point, one needs the expression for the slope of the isokine, which is obtained by taking differentials of the equation $\dot{k}$ = f(k) - nk - c:

(41) $d\dot{k}$ = f'(k)dk - ndk - dc.

Setting $d\dot{k}$ = 0, equation (41) is transformed into:

(42) dc = dk[f'(k) - n].

Rearranging terms yields the expression for the slope of the $\dot{k}$ = 0 isokine:

(43) dc/dk = [f'(k) - n].

Equation (43) shows that if f'(k) = n, dc/dk = 0. The slope would be positive, if f'(k) is greater than n, and vice versa.

The $\dot{c}$ = 0 isokine is derived from equation (35). The isokine is a vertical straight line at the point where f'(k) is equal to n. For larger values of k than k*, f'(k) is smaller than n and the term in the brackets of equation (35) is negative. Therefore $\dot{c}$ is negative.

For smaller values of k than k*, $\dot{c}$ is positive. These are the explanations for the negative sign (-) at the right-hand side of the straight vertical line and for the positive sign (+) at the left-hand side of the same line.

The relationship between these signs and the

isokine $\dot{k} = 0$ will be made clear if we look simultaneously at panel (B). It shows that for those values

of k greater than that of k*, $\dot{k} = 0$ and conversely.

Panel (C) shows that the isokines divide the phase
diagram into four quadrants. The directions of the dynamic movements of c and k are indicated by the arrows.
Only if c and k move along the paths indicated by the
heavy arrows will the system eventually attain the optimal growth path, which is denoted by the point E.
Otherwise, the dynamic process will diverge from E in
any of the directions indicated by the light arrows.
Hence, point E has the characteristics of "saddle-
point" stability.

References

Barone, E., "The Ministry of Production in the Collectivist State," in F.A. Hayek (ed.), Collectivist
Economic Planning (Routledge & Kegan Paul, 1935).

Baumol, W.J., Economic Theory and Operations Analysis
(Englewood Cliffs, N.J.: Prentice-Hall, 1977).

Burmeister, E. and Dobell, A.R., Mathematical Theories
of Economic Growth (London, England: Macmillan, 1970).

Dorfman, R., "An Economic Interpretation of Control
Theory," American Economic Review, Vol. LIX, No. 5,
December 1969.

Hadley, G. and Kemp, M.C., Variational Methods in
Economics (New York: American Elsevier Publishing
Co., Inc., 1971).

Hicks, J.F., Capital and Growth (New York: Oxford
University Press, 1965).

Intrilligator, M.D., Mathematical Optimization and
Economic Theory (Englewood Cliffs, N.J.: Prentice-
Hall, 1971).

Lange, O. and Taylor, F., On the Theory of Socialism
(University of Minnesota Press, 1938).

Phelps, E.S., Golden Rules of Economic Growth; Studies in Efficient and Optimal Investment (New York: Norton, 1966).

Pontryagin, L.S., Boltyanskii, V.G., Gamkrelidze, R.V., and Mishchenko, E.F., The Mathematical Theory of Optimal Process (New York: Interscience Publishers, John Wiley and Sons, Inc., 1962).

Robinson, J., Collected Economic Papers, Vol. III (Oxford: Blackwell, 1965).

Samuelson, P., Foundations of Economic Analysis (Cambridge, Mass.: Harvard University Press, 1958).

Takayama, A., Mathematical Economics (Hinsdale, Ill.: The Dryden Press, 1974).

Chapter 10

THEORETICAL HERITAGE OF THE ALTERNATIVE PARADIGM

The alternative paradigm in growth theory expounded by the critics of neoclassical theory may be viewed as an integration of several major strands in the history of economic thought. Among them, the salient approaches are those of: (a) Ricardo, (b) Marx, (c) Marshall, (d) Keynes, (e) Kalecki, (f) Harrod, and (g) von Neumann. We will briefly trace the influences of these respective approaches on the alternative growth theories.

(a) Ricardo highlighted the simple but essential relation connecting the distribution of income and the rate of profit to the rate of economic growth. He rejected supply and demand in the market place as determinants of income distribution, and instead, like other classical writers, explicitly included economic classes in his discussion of income distribution.[1] The Ricardian theory of the determination of the wage rate and the profit rate is the antithesis of neoclassical marginal productivity theory. For in his theory, the long-run equilibrium wage rate is exogenously given by the Malthusian theory of population; it has nothing to do with the marginal product of labor. Likewise, the rate of profit has no relation to the marginal product of capital. For the rate of profit cannot be determined until the share of profit is given first; i.e., given the institutionally determined relative shares and the exogenously given wage rate, relative prices will be determined by the competitive condition that the rate of profit must be uniform throughout the economy.[2]

---

[1] For penetrating analyses of the Ricardian system, see E.J. Nell, "Theories of Growth and Theories of Value," op. cit.; Robert V. Eagly, The Structure of Classical Economic Theory (New York: Oxford University Press, 1974), Chapter 3; Luigi L. Pasinetti, Growth and Income Distribution (London: Cambridge University Press, 1974), Chapter I; Maurice Dobb, Theories of Value and Distribution Since Adam Smith, op. cit., Chapter 3; and Mark Blaug, op. cit., Chapter 4.

[2] For definitive analysis of Ricardian value theory, see Piero Sraffa, Production of Commodities By Means of

Professor Nicholas Kaldor was the first to see that Keynes' and Harrod's hypotheses could be inserted into Ricardo's theoretical framework and thereby give birth to a new answer to the old Ricardian problem.[3] This synthesis is the "widow's cruse" theory of income distribution which will be considered in Chapter 12 of this book.

In discussing the significance of capital, Ricardo and the classical economists recognized capital's dual nature. They treated capital - as an input in the production sphere - purely as a technical problem, independent of any social relations; whereas they treated capital - as private property in the income distribution sphere - primarily in terms of its social relations.

(b) Marx admired the analytical skills of Ricardo but criticized him for lacking the concept of a "mode of

---

Commodities (London: Cambridge University Press, 1960). A simple illustration of the statement in the text is as follows: Suppose the economy consists of two industries: industry one and industry two. Prices are determined by the existing technology and distribution of income. The price equations are:

$$P_1 = \text{costs of production} = (a_{21}P_2)\,(1 + r) + a_{o1}w$$

$$P_2 = \text{costs of production} = (a_{12}P_1)\,(1 + r) + a_{o2}w$$

where P_1 and P_2 are the prices of industries one and two; a_{21} and a_{12} are the input coefficients; a_{21} means output of industry one required by industry two; a_{12} refers to output of industry one purchased by industry two; the rate of profit is r; a_{o1} and a_{o2} are labor input coefficients and w is the wage rate. Given the exogenously determined wage rate and the uniform rate of profit determined by competition, P_1 and P_2 are simultaneously determined.

[3]Nicholas Kaldor, "Alternative Theories of Distribution," Review of Economic Studies, Vol. 23 (March 1956), pp. 83-100. Also see Luigi L. Pasinetti, op. cit., Chapters 4 and 5.

production."[4] This deficiency in the Ricardian analysis,
as perceived by Marx, was the main reason why capital as
an input in the sphere of production was being treated
as asocial and purely technical. Conversely, the Marxian concept of a "mode of production" permeated the
social, political and intellectual life process in general. In the sphere of production, the social relationships involved could be specified by such characteristics
as organization of the production-process, division of
labor, authority and control. Ricardo and the classical economists failed to consider this aspect of the
social phenomenon. Furthermore, Marx made a distinction
between the term "labor" and "labor power." For, according to Marx, capitalist production was commodity
production extended to the point where labor-power had
also become a commodity. During the contractual period, a laborer was free to sell his "labor power." In
this period, there was bourgeois equality where no exploitation was involved in the sphere of exchange. But
the laborer did not own the means of production. Hence,
although he was initially free to choose the buyer of
his "labor power," the laborer could not subsequently
free himself from the capitalist as a whole since he
had to work for a capitalist. Here lay the despotism
of capital in the production sphere: it was a social
relationship and not just a technological consideration.
In order to highlight this despotism of capital in the
sphere of production, Marx made the distinction between
"constant" and "variable" capital. The former refers
to the means of production; the latter implied "labor
power." It was "variable" capital that created the
surplus, so the capitalist tried every way to reduce
"variable" capital and thus increase the surplus. As a

---

[4]For modern interpretations of Marxian economics, see
Michio Morishima, Marx's Economics: A Dual Theory of
Value and Growth (London: Cambridge University Press,
1973); Bob Rowthorn, "Neo-Ricardianism or Marxism?"
in New Left Review, London, England, Vol. 86, pp. 63-
87. Earlier interpretations of Marxian economics are
voluminous. We suggest the following: Joan Robinson,
An Essay on Marxian Economics (London: Macmillan, 1952);
Ernest Mandel, Marxist Economic Theory, translated by
Brian Pearce (New York: Monthly Review Press, 1968);
and David Horowitz edition, Marx and Modern Economics
(New York and London: Modern Reader Paperbacks, Monthly
Review Press, 1968).

result, tyranny of capital was the source of technological unemployment, the industrial reserve army of
unemployed, the increasing misery of the laboring
poor, the falling rate of profit, the concentration of
economic power, and class struggle. Thus, the social
relations (mode of production) involved in capital -
both in the sphere of distribution and in that of production - sowed the seed for the eventual breakdown
of capitalism.

The critics of neoclassical theory brought the
Marxian theory of exploitation to date in the guise
of a power struggle in collective bargaining to explain
the distribution of income.[5] However, they did not go
all the way with Marx. Thus, the New Left prefer to
call these critics "Neo-Ricardians."[6]

(c) Alfred Marshall believed that the Ricardian
cost-of-production theory of value was basically valid.
In his Principles of Economics (1891), he attempted to
reconcile the Ricardian principle with the concept of
subjective utility in the context of Darwinian evolutionary theory.[7] Although he was one of the founders
of the English neoclassical school, he deviated from
the neoclassical tradition by insisting that the short-
period supply or offer price should include a level of
profits in addition to the prime (variable) and supplementary (fixed) costs. He wrote:

> . . . the true marginal supply price for short
> periods . . . is nearly always above, and gen-
> erally very much above the special or prime
> cost for raw materials, labour and wear-and-
> tear of plant, which is immediately and dir-
> ectly involved by getting a little further
> use out of appliances which are not fully em-

---

[5]See Amit Bhaduri, "The Concept of the Marginal Productivity of Capital and the Wicksell Effect," Oxford Economic
Papers, Vol. XVIII, No. 3, 1966, pp. 284-88; Joan Robinson, "A Reconsideration of the Theory of Value," Collected
Economic Papers, Vol. III (Oxford: Basil Blackwell, 1965),
pp. 173-81; and Edward J. Nell, op. cit.

[6]Bob Rowthorn, op. cit.

[7]Marshall pointed out: "In this matter economists have
much to learn from the recent experiences of biology: and
Darwin's profound discussions of the question throw a

ployed.[8]

The Marshallian short-period supply price was accepted by Keynes in both his Treatise on Money (1930) and The General Theory (1936). Consequently, it was formulated more precisely by Michael Kalecki in his Theory of Economic Dynamics (1952) by the concept of a mark-up (reflecting the "degree of monopoly") over prime and supplementary costs. In this manner, Marshall's supply price concept is the intellectual antecedent of the Robinsonian and Kaldorian theories of prices.

(d) Keynes' works provided important building blocks for the growth models of Joan Robinson, Kaldor, and Pasinetti. His well-known passage on profits being likened to a "widow's cruse" in Treatise on Money was[9] the origin of the Kaldorian theory of distribution; his aggregate demand and supply analysis in The General Theory provided the point of departure for the different versions of Neo-Ricardian dynamic economics. The basic differences between two of these versions by Joan Robinson and Nicholas Kaldor will be examined in Chapters 12 and 13 of this book.

---

strong light on the difficulties before us." Principles of Economics, 8th edition (New York: Macmillan, 1953), p. 50.

[8] Op. cit., pp. 374-5.

[9] J.M. Keynes, Treatise on Money, Vol. I (London: Macmillan, 1930), p. 139. Keynes wrote: ". . . Thus profits, as a source of capital increment for enterpreneurs, are a widow's cruse which remains undepleted however much of them may be devoted to riotous living. When on the other hand, enterpreneurs are making losses, and seek to recoup these losses by curtailing their normal expenditures on consumption, i.e., by saving more, the cruse becomes a Danaid jar which can never be filled up; for the effect of this reduced expenditure is to inflict on the producers of consumption-goods a loss of an equal amount. Thus the diminution of their wealth as a class is as great, in spite of their savings, as it was before."

(e) Michael Kalecki's contributions to the Post-Keynesian (Neo-Ricardian) theory are equally important as those of Keynes.[10] In the first place, Kalecki emphasized the monopolistic elements in the determination of prices and the Marxian class struggle's reflection in the size of the mark-up. Both Joan Robinson and Kaldor adopt similar positions. Secondly, Kalecki believed that savings and profits are determined by the change in the rate of investment. He wrote: "Profits will . . . be a function both of current investment and of investment in the near past; or roughly speaking, profits follow investment with a time lag. We can thus write as an approximate equation: $P_t = f(I_t - w)$ where w is the time lag involved."[11] This equation represents the theoretical underpinning of the Kaldorian "widow's cruse" theory of distribution.

Thirdly, Kalecki provided three important foundations for Joan Robinson's theories: (1) his emphasis on the primary importance of institutional factors behind the rate of growth is reflected in Joan Robinson's insistence on building a "historical model";[12] (2) his view that the long-run trend has no independent existence from the short period situations is clearly translated in her belief that no viable distinction can be made be-

---

[10]Michael Kalecki learned his economics from Marx. His most important works are collected in Selected Essays on the Dynamics of the Capitalist Economy (New York: Cambridge University Press, 1971). Excellent discussions of Kalecki's theory are given by J.A. Kregel in his Rate of Profit, Distribution and Growth: Two Views (Chicago and New York: Aldine, Atherton, 1971), pp. 99-103, J.A. Kregel, "Some Post-Keynesian Distribution Theory" in Sidney Weintraub edition, Modern Economic Thought (Philadelphia: University of Pennsylvania Press, 1977), Chapter 21, and A. Asimakopulos, "Post-Keynesian Growth Theory" in Modern Economic Thought, op. cit., Chapter 19.

[11]Michael Kalecki, Theory of Economic Dynamics (New York and London, Modern Reader Paperbacks, 1968), p. 54.

[12]Joan Robinson points out: "In an historical model, causal relations have to be specified. Today is a break in time between an unknown future and an irrevocable past. What happens next will result from the interactions of the behavior of human beings within the economy. Movement can

tween "short-run theory" and "long-run theory";[13] and
(3) his statement in his Outline of a Theory of the
Business Cycle (1933) is the foundation for the Robinson double-sided relationship between profits and investment.[14]

(f) As mentioned earlier in Chapter 2 of this book,
Harrod's model provided the point of departure for both
the neoclassical and the alternative post-Keynesian approaches to growth theory. In particular, the relation
between the Harrodian analysis and that of the Neo-
Ricardians is best summarized by Luigi L. Pasinetti and
A. Asimakopulos. Beginning with Pasinetti: "If Harrod-
Domar hypotheses are inserted into Ricardo's theoretical
scheme and proper account is taken of Keynes' effective
demand requirements for full employment, we are led back
to the old Ricardian problem of income distribution but
with an entirely new answer. Nicholas Kaldor was the
first to see this clearly."[15] Turning to Asimakopulos:
"Post-Keynesian growth theory has been woven from
various strands found mainly in the writings of John
Maynard Keynes and Michael Kalecki. Stimulated by
Harrod's approach, the theory places more emphasis on
income distribution."[16] Furthermore, the Harrodian
natural rate of growth (golden age path) provided the
Neo-Ricardians with the basic framework of analysis.
Their models are designed to explain the necessary conditions for golden age growth. Nonetheless, the limi-
tations of these models are fully recognized by Joan

---

only be forward." Essays on the Theory of Economic
Growth (New York: St. Martin's Press, Inc., 1962), p. 26.

[13]A. Asimakopulos, op. cit., pp. 370-1.

[14]A. Asimakopulos, op. cit., p. 383 n. Joan Robinson's
double-sided relationship between profits and investment
will be discussed in Chapter 12 of this volume.

[15]Luigi L. Pasinetti, Growth and Income Distribution:
Essays in Economic Theory (London: Cambridge University
Press, 1974), p. 97.

[16]A. Asimakopulos, op. cit., p. 369.

Robinson, who cautions:

> In reality, disturbing events occur on
> disequilibrium paths. The resulting
> turbulence is beyond the skill of model
> builders to analyze.[17]

Hence, while using Harrod's model as scaffolding, Joan
Robinson constructed her model to make comparisons between economies - each growing at a different golden
age rate - instead of explaining how economies traverse
from a disequilibrium to an equilibrium growth path.

(g) The von Neumann model not only was the first
rigorous model in nonaggregative capital theory, but
also contained the germ of the Kaldor-Robinson-Pasin-
etti theory of the rate of profit.[18] The von Neumann
rate of profit was determined neither by the marginal
efficiency of investment nor by the marginal productivity of capital. It was determined by the rate of
expansion of the system. Joan Robinson observed:
"Von Neumann assumed that the whole surplus was continuously being invested in enlarging the stock of commodities and increasing employment. Then total net profit
and total net investment are identically the same thing.
The rate of profit is equal to the rate of growth."[19]
Further considerations of the von Neumann approach to
economic growth will be taken up immediately in the
Appendix of this chapter.

---

[17]Joan Robinson, op. cit., p. 27.

[18]For an excellent nonmathematical interpretation of
the von Neumann model, see D.G. Champernowne, "A Note
on J. v. Neumann's Article on 'A Model of Economic
Equilibrium,'" Review of Economic Studies, Vol. 13,
1945-46, pp. 10-18.

[19]Joan Robinson, Economic Heresies (New York: Basic
Books, Inc., Publishers, 1971), p. 42.

References

Asimakopulos, A., "Post-Keynesian Growth Theory," in
S. Weintraub (ed.), Modern Economic Thought
(Philadelphia: University of Pennsylvania Press,
1977).

Bhaduri, A., "The Concept of the Marginal Productivity
of Capital and the Wicksell Effect," Oxford
Economic Papers, Vol. XVIII, No. 3, 1966.

Blaug, M., Economic Theory in Retrospect, 2nd Edition
(London: Heinemann, 1968).

Champernowne, D.G., "A Note on J. v. Neumann's Article
on 'A Model of Economic Equilibrium,'" Review of
Economic Studies, Vol. 13, 1945-46.

Dobb, M., Theories of Value and Distribution Since
Adam Smith (

Eagly, R.V., The Structure of Classical Economic Theory
(New York: Oxford University Press, 1974).

Horowitz, D. (ed.), Marx and Modern Economics (New York
and London: Modern Reader Paperbacks, Monthly
Review Press, 1968).

Kaldor, N., "Alternative Theories of Distribution,"
Review of Economic Studies, Vol. 23, March 1956.

Kalecki, M., Theory of Economic Dynamics (New York and
London: Modern Reader Paperbacks, 1968).

_____, Selected Essays on the Dynamics of the
Capitalistic Economy (New York: Cambridge University Press, 1971).

Keynes, J.M., Treatise on Money, Vol. I (London: Macmillan, 1930).

Kregel, J.A., Rate of Profit, Distribution and Growth:
Two Views (London and New York: Aldine-Atherton,
1971).

_____, "Some Post-Keynesian Distribution Theory,"
in S. Weintraub (ed.), Modern Economic Thought
(Philadelphia: University of Pennsylvania Press,
1977).

Mandel, E., _Marxist Economic Theory_ (New York: Monthly Review Press, 1968).

Marshall, A., _Principles of Economics_, 8th Edition (New York: Macmillan, 1953).

Morishima, M., _Marx's Economics: A Dual Theory of Value and Growth_ (London: Cambridge University Press, 1973).

Nell, E.J., "Theories of Growth and Theories of Value," _Economic Development and Cultural Change_, Vol. XVI, 1967.

Pasinetti, L.L., _Growth and Income Distribution: Essays in Economic Theory_ (London: Cambridge University Press, 1974).

Robinson, J., _An Essay on Marxian Economics_ (London: Macmillan, 1952).

_____, _Essays on the Theory of Economic Growth_ (New York: St. Martin's Press, Inc., 1962).

_____, _Collected Economic Papers_, Vol. III (Oxford: Basil Blackwell, 1965).

_____, _Economic Heresies_ (New York: Basic Books, Inc., Publishers, 1971).

Rowthorn, B., "Neo-Ricardianism or Marxism?," _New Left Review_, London, England, Vol. 86.

Sraffa, P., _Production of Commodities By Means of Commodities_ (London: Cambridge University Press, 1960).

APPENDIX

The von Neumann Model of General Economic Equilibrium

The von Neumann model is a normative growth model
that deals with an economy which is expanding as a
whole over time at a uniform geometric rate.[1]

The Neumannian economy has the following properties:

1. It is a closed economy, a pure production system where goods are produced from each other in a circular fashion by processes of the fixed-coefficient
type. A finite number of goods, n, is produced by m
processes, with the possibility that m $>$ n.

The time dimension is introduced into the model by
making each process of production take exactly one unit
of time, and by considering the output of each period
as the input variable for the next period. The model
allows for the possibility of alternative processes,
intermediate goods and joint production. Natural factors of production are assumed to be in unlimited supply, and constant returns to scale and competitive conditions are assumed to prevail.

2. There is no final demand in the Neumannian
economy. Labor is produced by the households who
perform work in return for the necessities of life such
as food, shelter and clothing. Thus, the worker-con-
sumer role is reduced to that of a farm animal. Although a dehumanizing assumption, this has the merit
of pointing out that prices are determined on the supply side only and not by the interaction of supply
and demand.

3. Saving out of wages is assumed to be zero,
while income in excess of wages, i.e., profits, is
assumed to be saved and reinvested.

---

[1]Champernowne calls this a quasi-stationary rather than
a stationary state mainly because of the "uniform expansion of the whole system. . . under equilibrium."

121

With these assumptions in the background, the model is designed to answer the following questions: (1) which processes will be used; (2) what the relative velocity will be with which the total quantity of goods increase; (3) what prices will obtain; and (4) what the rate of interest will be.

The answer to the first question hinges upon profitability. With competitive conditions, given prices and the interest rate, the only processes used are those which yield zero profits. To go into the details, let $a_{ij} \geq 0$ (i = 1,2 . . ., n and j = 1, 2, . . . m) to be the quantity of inputs used in process P_j to produce $b_{ij} \geq 0$ of the n goods. These processes are used at certain intensities $x_i \geq 0$ where $x_i = 0$ means that process P_i is not used. The supply of any good at time t is simply the output of that good obtained from each process. Thus, for the ith good the available supply can be denoted $\sum_{j=1}^{m} b_{ij} x_j (t)$. The supply of all goods at time t constitutes the input used to produce output for the period t + 1. Technically it is not possible to consume more than the available supply, i.e., the input for the period t + 1 cannot exceed the available output at time t. In matrix notation this constraint can be stated as:

(1) $\underline{A}\ \underline{X}\ (t + 1) \leqq \underline{B}\ \underline{X}\ (t)$ where

$$A = \begin{bmatrix} a_{11} & a_{12} & \cdots & a_{1m} \\ a_{21} & a_{22} & \cdots & a_{2m} \\ \cdots & \cdots & & \\ a_{n1} & a_{n2} & & a_{nm} \end{bmatrix} \quad B = \begin{bmatrix} b_{11} & b_{12} & \cdots & b_{1m} \\ b_{21} & b_{22} & \cdots & b_{2m} \\ \cdots & \cdots & & \\ b_{n1} & b_{n2} & & b_{nm} \end{bmatrix}$$

$$X = \begin{bmatrix} x_1 \\ x_2 \\ : \\ : \\ x_m \end{bmatrix}$$

Since production takes time, the profitability of any process is determined by comparing the costs of production that are incurred at time t to the revenues that flow at time t + 1 discounted to time t by the market interest rate. Thus, if we denote the price of any good as y_i and the interest rate as r, we get the following constraint:

(2) $(1 + r)$ $\underline{A}$ $\underline{Y}$ $\geq$ $\underline{B}$ $\underline{Y}$ where $\underline{Y} = [Y_1, Y_2, \ldots, Y_n]$.

If in (2) strict inequality holds for any process, then that process will not be used; i.e., its intensity will be zero, since it will be operating at a loss in that case.

Von Neumann's definition of equilibrium provides the answer to the second question. He defines equilibrium as a state of balanced growth in which the intensities of all processes remain the same while growing at a constant rate, α. In such a state prices and the interest rate remain constant. He defines α as the rate of growth of the slowest growing good and any good that grows faster than α becomes a free good as we shall explain below.

Symbolically this can be written as:

(3) $\underline{X}$ $(t + 1) = (1 + \alpha)$ $\underline{X}(t)$

The essence of this formulation is to point out that in equilibrium, the system of production used is that which has the greatest rate of growth among all possible production systems.

Substituting (3) in (1) we get

(4) $(1 + \alpha)$ $\underline{A} X(t) \leq \underline{B} X(t)$

Now, if in (4) inequality holds for any good, meaning that output of that good exceeds input by more than α, then that particular good becomes a free good with a price of zero. This result provides the answer to the third question. Viewing it as a linear programming problem, (4) and (2) could be considered as the primal and the dual of the problem so that whenever a strict inequality holds in either of them then the corresponding dual variable will be zero.

Now that the scope of the model is clearer, we can identify the unknowns as n goods, m processes, the interest rate r, and the rate of growth α. These add up to n + m + 2 unknowns. But since we are interested only in relative prices and intensities the number of unknowns becomes n + m. Since in general m > n, von Neumann relied on Brouwer's Fixed-Point theorem to reach the solution to the model: For the system of equations (2) and (4) to have an economic meaning at least one equality should hold in each system. Thus, in equilibrium, mul-

123

tiplying (2) by X(t) and (5) by Y yields the following equilibrium equations:

(2') $(1 + r) \underline{A} \underline{X}(t) \underline{Y} = \underline{B} \underline{X}(t) \underline{Y}$

(4') $(1 + \alpha) \underline{A} \underline{X}(t) \underline{Y} = \underline{B} \underline{X}(t) \underline{Y}$

From (2') and (4'), it is clear that

$$r^* = \alpha^* = \frac{\underline{B} \underline{X}(t)\underline{Y}}{\underline{A} \underline{X}(t)\underline{Y}} - 1$$

This says that in equilibrium there exists a minimum rate of interest r*, and a maximum rate of balanced growth α * where the rate of interest is equal to the rate of growth. Hence, the fourth question is answered.

References

von Neumann, J., "A Model of General Economic Equilibrium," Review of Economic Studies, Vol. XIII, No. 33, 1945-1946.

Chapter 11

RESWITCHING AND CAPITAL-REVERSING
CONTROVERSY IN THE THEORY OF CAPITAL

It will be recalled that neoclassical capital theory
has been considered in Chapter 3 of this book. Following Ferguson, the theory is shown as an integral part of
the beautiful edifice of neoclassical theory erected
upon the foundations of the linearly homogeneous production function and input-output pricing processes.
To put it differently, Robert Solow gives what he calls
the "highbrow" answer to the question of the proper
scope of capital theory as follows:

> The highbrow answer is that the theory of
> capital is after all just a part of the funda-
> mentally microeconomic theory of allocation
> of resources, necessary to allow for the fact
> that commodities can be transformed into
> other commodities over time. Just as the
> theory of resource allocation has its "dual"
> a theory of competitive pricing, so the
> theory of capital has its "dual" a theory of
> intertemporal pricing involving rentals, in-
> terest rates, present values and the like.
> In both cases, a complete price theory is
> also a theory of distribution among factors
> of production, if not among persons.[1]

The neoclassical analysis of capital is conducted
in terms of supply and demand for a scarce resource.
Behind the supply of capital (the supply of savings)
is the theory of consumer's choice between current and
future consumption; behind the demand for new capital
(demand for savings) is the concept of net productivity
of capital. The rate of interest plays the crucial role
in both the supply and demand sides of the model. The
practical policy implication of neoclassical capital
theory is that a reduced interest rate always brings
with it a more capital-intensive technique of production, which in the long run leads to increased produc-

---

[1]Robert M. Solow, Capital Theory and the Rate of Return
(Chicago: Rand McNally & Co., 1965), p. 14.

tivity of labor and a higher real wage rate. Consequently, the material standard of living also rises.
This policy implication is revealed by the "parable"
that there is an association between a lower real rate
of interest (which, in equilibrium, is equal to the
rate of profit) and a higher value of capital per man.

The members of the Anglo-Italian school attacked
both the neoclassical theory of the supply of savings
and that of the choice of investment technique. Following Keynes, they attacked the supply side by arguing
that the rate of interest was not an important determinant of savings. In their view, savings were determined by institutional factors such as the "degree of
monopoly" and the conflict between income classes.
Clearly, integrating these arguments, the "widow's
cruse" theory of distribution was the Anglo-Italian
counterpart to the neoclassical theory of the supply
of savings.

The Neo-Ricardians' attack on the demand side of
capital theory was actually an indirect challenge to
the entire neoclassical theory of prices. The major
weapon of the attack - the capital-reversing and -
reswitching controversy - was intended to undermine
the neoclassical parable, relating low profit rates
with high values of capital per man, and its corollary
parable, the marginal productivity theory of distribution.

The phenomena of capital-reversing and - reswitching (or double switching) were first noticed by
Joan Robinson, Champernowne and Sraffa.[2] However, the
origin of their discussions may be traced back to
Wicksell and probably, to Ricardo.

---

[2]See Joan Robinson, "The Production Function and the
Theory of Capital," in Collected Economic Papers, Vol.
2 (Oxford: Blackwell, 1965), pp. 114-31. First pub-
lished in Review of Economic Studies, Vol. 21, 1953-4,
pp. 81-106 and Joan Robinson, Accumulation of Capital
(London: Macmillan, 1956); D.G. Champernowne, "The
Production Function and the Theory of Capital: A
Comment," Review of Economic Studies, Vol. 21, 1953-4,
pp. 112-35; and Piero Sraffa, Production of Commodities
By Means of Commodities (London: Cambridge Univ. Press, 1960

The "Wicksell Effect"

In his restatement of the capital theory of Eugen Bohm-Bawerk,[3] Wicksell discovered that the marginal productivity concept cannot be applied to capital and that for the economy as a whole the marginal productivity of capital is smaller than the rate of interest.[4] Wicksell's finding is now commonly known as the "Wicksell effect." A modified version of the Wicksellian mathematical formulation of the Austrian capital theory is as follows:[5]

$$(1) \quad y = f(\Upsilon)$$

Equation (1) states that output per man (y) is a function of the average period of production which is denoted by the symbol Υ. The meaning of Υ will be made clear by the following equations.

$$(2) \quad S = wL\,\Upsilon$$

$$(3) \quad \Upsilon = \frac{S}{wL}$$

Equation (2) is a definition of circulating capital (a subsistence fund analogous to the classical wages fund) which is represented by the symbol S. In the same equation, the symbol w stands for the real wage per man and L denotes the number of workers employed. Equation (3) is an explanation of the average period of production which shows the average period of time in which input is "frozen" or "retained" in the production process. The ratio $\frac{S}{wL}$ on the right-hand side of equation (3) shows the amount of given circulating capital invested divided by the flow of wage payment.[6] Thus,

---

[3] Eugen von Bohm-Bawerk, The Positive Theory of Capital (1889). English translation Libertarian Press, South Holland, Ill., 1959.

[4] Knut Wickwell, Lectures on Political Economy (London: Routledge & Kegan Paul, Ltd., 1934); and Value, Capital and Rent, trans. S.H. Frowien (New York, 1954).

[5] For a more in-depth discussion of the Wicksellian model, see Mark Blaug, Economic Theory in Retrospect, op. cit., Chapter 12; and Friedrich A. Lutz, The Theory of Interest (Chicago: Aldine Publishing Co., 1966), Chaps. 1 and 2.

[6] In capital theory, this case is called "the flow input-point output" case. In this case capital is limited to circulating capital which is regarded as goods in process.

the average period of production depends upon the size of working or circulating capital and the wage bill during the production period. A lengthening of the average production period requires the increase of circulating capital. It should be noted that the Austrians used the concepts of average period of production and subsistence fund as simplifying devices to bypass the vexing problem of measurement of heterogeneous capital stock. Their objective was to highlight the round-about process (time consuming process) of production. This process also requires the condition that labor be applied continuously throughout the production period.

Equation (2) in per capita terms is written as follows:

$$(4) \quad k = \frac{S}{L} = w\tau$$

where the symbol k stands for subsistence fund per man $\frac{S}{L}$. Differentiating equation (4) with respect to τ, we have:

$$(5) \quad \frac{dk}{d\tau} = \tau \frac{dw}{d\tau} + w\frac{d\tau}{d\tau} = \tau \frac{dw}{d\tau} + w$$

Rearranging terms, we obtain:

$$(6) \quad w = \frac{dk}{d\tau} - \tau \frac{dw}{d\tau}$$

For the individual entrepreneur under perfect competition (i.e., the individual entrepreneur is a price-taker in both the output and factor markets),

$$\frac{dw}{d\tau} = 0, \text{ and thus}$$

$$(7) \quad w = \frac{dk}{d\tau}$$

i.e., the amount of increased circulating capital per man required by the individual entrepreneur for a lengthening of the production process is equal to the real wage rate. Consequently, at the microeconomic level, the rate of profit in equilibrium is equal to the marginal product of capital. This conclusion is reached in the following way:

$$(8) \quad y = w + r(w\tau)$$

This equation states the costs of production for y. The symbol r refers to the rate of profit (rate of return to capital) and the expression $w\tau$ stands for the circulating capital per man invested in the production process. Rearranging terms, we have the equation defining the rate of profit:

$$(9) \quad r = \frac{y - w}{w\tau}, \text{ or } (9') \quad k = w\tau = \frac{y - w}{r}.$$

Equation (9') denotes the value of capital.

Given the real wage rate, the individual entrepreneur chooses the optimal average period of production (in modern terminology, this means the choice of optimal technique) so as to maximize the rate of profit. Accordingly, we differentiate equation (9) with respect to τ and set $\frac{dr}{d\tau} = 0$:

$$(10) \quad \frac{dr}{d\tau} = \frac{w\tau \cdot \frac{dy}{d\tau} - (y - w)\frac{dw\tau}{d\tau}}{(w\tau)^2} = 0$$

Rearranging terms, we obtain:

$$(11) \quad \frac{1}{w\tau}\frac{dy}{d\tau} = \frac{w(y - w)}{(w\tau)^2}$$

Multiplying both sides of equation (11) by the expression $w\tau$, we have:

$$(12) \quad \frac{dy}{d\tau} = \frac{w(y-w)}{w\tau} = \frac{y - w}{\tau}$$

Utilizing equation (12), equation (9) can be restated as:

$$(13) \quad r = \frac{y - w}{w\tau} = \frac{\frac{dy}{d\tau}}{w}$$

Substituting $w = \frac{dk}{d\tau}$ into equation (13), the desired result is obtained:

$$(14) \quad r = \frac{\frac{dy}{d\tau}}{\frac{dk}{d\tau}} = \frac{dy}{d\tau}$$

where $\frac{dy}{d\tau}$ stands for the marginal product of capital.

129

However, Wickwell discovered that this equality
does not hold at the macroeconomic level. For the
economic system as a whole, the increased amount of
circulating capital required for lengthening the
average period of production would be larger than the
real wage payment as depicted by equation (6). It
follows that the rate of profit in equilibrium would
exceed the marginal social product of capital. This
conclusion is arrived at by substituting equation (6)
into equation (13):

$$(15) \quad r = \frac{\frac{dy}{d\tau}}{\frac{dk}{d\tau} - \tau \frac{dw}{d\tau}}$$

The denominator $\frac{dk}{d\tau} - \tau \frac{dw}{d\tau}$ on the right-hand side of

equation (15) states that a portion of the increased
circulating capital per man would be absorbed by the
rise in the real wage rate associated with a fall in
the rate of profit. Thus, Joan Robinson observes:
"Wicksell points out that the length of the period of
production does not by itself determine the ratio of
capital to labor, because the value of capital required
for a given method of production depends on the real-
wage rate."[7] Another reason for this phenomenon is
that the fall in the rate of profit which is equal to the
rate of interest in equilibrium would lead to a revaluation of the entire capital stock - both new and existing
capital. This is the "Wicksell effect." G.C. Harcourt
writes:

> In the modern literature the "real" and
> "financial" aspects of an increase in so-
> cial capital have come to be discussed
> under the heading of real and price Wick-
> sell effects, respectively.

---

[7]Joan Robinson, The Accumulation of Capital, op. cit., p.
396. She further observes: " . . . this point of Wicksell's is the key to the whole theory of accumulation and
of the determination of wages and profits." p. 396. However, T.W. Swan argues: "To its discoverer, the Wicksell
effect seemed mainly important as an obstacle to the ac-
ceptance of 'von Thunen's thesis,' the marginal productivity theory of interest." To Swan, "The Wicksell effect
is nothing but an inventory revaluation"; and it is not
"the key to the whole theory of accumulation." See Swan's
"Economic Growth and Capital Accumulation," Economic Record, Vol. 32, 1956, pp. 343-61.

The price Wicksell effect relates to changes in the value of capital as w and r change their values but techniques do not change, i.e., it is associated with the w-r relationship that corresponds to one technique. Real Wicksell effects relate to changes in the value of capital associated with changes in techniques as w and r take on different values, i.e., they are differences in the values of capital at (or, rather, very near) switch points on the envelope of the w-r relationship.

The "price Wicksell effect" referred to by Harcourt may be illustrated by equation (9'):

$$k = w\,\Upsilon = \frac{y - w}{r}\;.$$

The implication of this equation is that valuation of capital, or the determination of capital intensity, requires that w and r be first specified. This is the contention of Joan Robinson in the capital-reversing and - reswitching debate. In other words, the value of k is not independent of distribution.[9] Wicksell himself was not fully aware of this implication. Hence, one may say that in his restatement of the Austrian capital theory, Wicksell stumbled into the capital-reversing and reswitching phenomena.[10]

Piero Sraffa's Contributions to the Controversy

The main concern of Piero Sraffa's important book, Production of Commodities By Means of Commodities, was to solve the Ricardian problem of finding an "invariable measure of value."[11] Sraffa solved the problem by constructing a "standard composite commodity." Although his definitive solution is beyond our purview in this

---

[9]This is the Ricardian problem of finding an "invariable measure of value" independent of distribution.

[10]Joan Robinson herself also stumbled into the phenomena. She writes: "For my part, I only became aware that Wicksell had made the point after I had stumbled upon it myself. It is mentioned by C.G. Uhr ('Wicksell, A Centennial Evaluation,' American Economic Review, Dec. 1951), who calls it Wicksell effect." Joan Robinson, op. cit., p. 391 n.

[11]Piero Sraffa, Production of Commodities By Means of Commodities: Prelude to a Critique of Economic Theory (London: Cambridge University Press, 1960).

section, we shall take up his separate concerns of the choice of techniques of production and the possibility of reswitching them. "It is in this exposition," J.A. Kregel points out, "that Sraffa's 'critique' of existing economic theory (as suggested by the subtitle of his book) is most explicit."[12] For Sraffa has demonstrated that it is impossible to determine the value of capital or capital intensity independently of the rate of profit. This conclusion obviously refuted the neoclassical claim that the rate of profit (the marginal product of capital) could be explained independently of the valuation of capital.

In the spirit of Ricardo and Marx, Sraffa treated capital goods as indirect labor. To him, each technique of production was comprised of direct and indirect labor, the latter being the specific capital requirements associated with the technique. Sraffa converted the indirect labor into direct labor through a process of "reduction to dated quantity of labor."[13] This conversion process involved netting out the direct labor from the capital components regressively through the various phases of construction. Whatever indirect labor remained from this reduction process eventually became negligible. Therefore, the costs of production of any technique could be represented by all the past labor properly dated and valued. However, a rate of interest (profit) had to be assigned to converted direct labor in the costs equation. For capital required time and the money tied up in its creation had to be compensated for by the rate of interest. In addition, Sraffa pointed out that techniques of production within a spectrum could be ranked in terms of their costs of capital per man required. In a stationary state, the costs of capital per man for a technique could be written:

$$k = \frac{y - w}{r} .[14]$$

[12] J.A. Kregel, Two Views, op. cit., p. 35.

[13] Piero Sraffa, op. cit., Chapter 6.

[14] For more in-depth discussions, see G.C. Harcourt, Some Cambridge Controversies, op. cit., Appendix to Chapter 4 and p. 40; and J.A. Kregel, Two Views, op. cit., pp. 18-39; also J.A. Kregel, The Reconstruction of Political Economy: An Introduction to Post-Keynesian Economics (New York: John Wiley & Sons, 1973), Chapter 7.

Sraffa's critique of neoclassical capital theory
was succinctly and masterfully summarized by Paul A.
Samuelson as follows:[15]

Suppose there are two ways (techniques) of making
a commodity. Method A requires 7 units of labor 2 periods before the final output is produced. Method B requires 2 units of labor 3 periods earlier and 6 labor
units 1 period earlier. Which method is more roundabout and time-intensive? Sraffa argued that there was
no technological way to say which was more time-intensive.
If this were true, the compound-interest effect of changes
in the interest rate would destroy the neoclassical parable that a lower r elicits a more roundabout method of
production.

To understand the compound-interest effect, first
suppose the interest rate were very small. At this low
interest rate, method A is cheaper than B since $7 < 6 + 2$.
Alternatively, suppose the interest rate were very high -
say, 200 per cent. In this case, merely compounding 2
labor units for 3 periods makes B's method much more
costly than A's, compounding 7 for 2 periods. So again,
at a very high rate of interest, method A is preferred.
However, at all interest rates, say between 50 and 100
per cent, method B is cheaper. In brief, as the interest
rate increases linearly, from a very low to a very high
rate, we encounter first the switching of techniques from
A to B and then the reswitching from B to A.

"Sraffa has, at this point, provided the first direct
proof of the primal role of the rate of profits in the
economic analysis of capital theory," observes Kregel.
"In his exposition of reduction to dated labour, he has
demonstrated that the valuation of capital is impossible
without reference to the distribution implied in the
rate of profits."[16]

---

[15]Paul A. Samuelson, Economics (New York: McGraw-Hill,
1973), 9th edition, pp. 615-17.

[16]J.A. Kregel, Two Views, op. cit., p. 31.

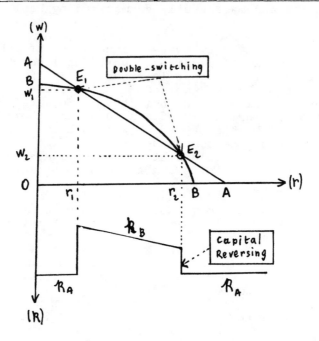

Figure 32

The upper portion of Figure 32 shows the familiar w-r relationship. Technique A is represented by a straight line which implies what Harcourt calls "neutral price Wicksell effect."[18] By that, Harcourt means that the value of k is constant despite differences in the value of r. Figure 33a illustrates this point. On the other hand, in Figure 33b, technique B is depicted by a curve which is concave to the origin. This implies a "negative price Wicksell effect," which shows that the value of k is lower, the lower is the value of r.

---

[17]G.C. Harcourt, op. cit., p. 126, Figure 4.1.

[18]G.C. Harcourt, op. cit., pp. 40-45.

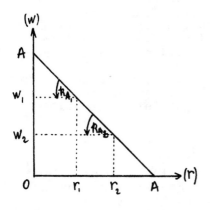

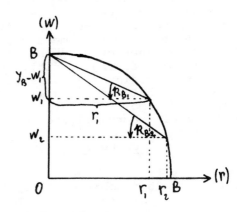

Figure 33a   Figure 33b

The two intersection points, E_1 and E_2, in Figure 32
are the switch points. Only at the switch points are w
and r the same for both techniques. The relation of the
value of k to different rates of interest is shown in the
lower portion of Figure 32. It shows that for values of
r greater than r_2, the costs of Technique A will be less

than those of B. Hence, A will be selected over B. However, Technique B will be cheaper than A at all interest
rates between r_1 and r_2. Thus, the profit-maximizing

producer will then choose B over A. Since technique A is
the more mechanized process (the labor equipped with A is
more productive than that equipped with B[19]), the shift
means capital-reversing. This is Joan Robinson's "Ruth
Cohen Curiosum."[20]

---

[19]This point may be illustrated as follows: In a stationary state, the value of k_A may be written as $k_A = \dfrac{y_A - w}{r}$

where k_A denotes the value of capital per man for technique

A. In the same vein, $k_B = \dfrac{y_B - w}{r}$. Rearranging terms,
$y_A = w + rk_A$ and $y_B = w + rk_B$.
If r equals zero, $(y_A = w_1) > (y_B = w)$. This is reflected in
Figure 32 on the vertical axis: we see that point A is higher than B.

[20]Joan Robinson, op. cit., pp. 109-110.

135

Figure 32 further shows that for values of r below r_1, once again technique A becomes cheaper. Consequently, a reswitching to the more mechanized technique will take place. Both these phenomena of capital-reversing and re-switching are depicted by the lower portion of Figure 32. The capital-reversing possibility exposed the Achilles heel of the neoclassical parable that there is an invariant relation between r and k. If this invariant, keystone relation is demolished, all of the beautiful edifice of neoclassical theory will be tottering.

Samuelson's Summing Up

The criticism of neoclassical parables was formally launched by Joan Robinson in 1953.[21] She was subsequently joined in the debate by Luigi L. Pasinetti, Pierangelo Garegnani, David Levhari, Paul A. Samuelson, Michio Mori-shima, Michael Bruno, Edwin Burmeister, Etyan Shehinski and others.[22] However, Joan Robinson's main interest was not the problem of capital measurement per se. Rather, the central issue she raised along with the "Anglo-Italian" school concerned the answer to the question: "Do we develop a 'better' theory of economic growth by extending Keynes or Walras into the dynamics of the long run?"[23] This central issue will be considered in the following chapters.

---

[21]Joan Robinson, "The Production Function and the Theory of Capital" in her Collected Economic Papers, Vol. 2, op. cit., pp. 114-31.

[22]See "Paradoxes in Capital Theory: A Symposium" in Quarterly Journal of Economics, Vol. LXXX, Nov. 1966 No. 4. A thorough review of the issues involved, with references to the key articles in the controversy is to be found in G.C. Harcourt, Some Cambridge Controversies, op. cit.

[23]These are the words of Thomas K. Rymes. See his On Concepts of Capital and Technical Change (London: Cambridge University Press, 1971), p. 1. T.K. Rymes writes: "The Cambridge controversy, as it may be called, has a number of foci of disagreement, viz. (i) Should full employment be assumed or generated by the analysis? (ii) What are the assumed properties of the investment behaviour of entre-preneurs? (iii) Which savings assumptions - neoclassical or Anglo-Italian - should be employed? (iv) What is the relevance of steady-state equilibrium analysis when econ-omic growth results from a sequence of short-run decisions - the only 'run' in which decisions can be made? (v) What role, if any, does money play in the process of economic growth?" p. 1.

As for the reswitching debate, both of the opposing sides relinquished some ground from their polar positions.

After his valiant defense of the neoclassical parables,[24] Samuelson in 1973 made the following statement:

> The science of political economy has not yet the empirical knowledge to decide whether the real world is nearer to the idealized polar cases represented by (a) the neoclassical parable, or (b) the simple reswitching paradigm.

> In conclusion, the economic concepts that all can agree on, regardless of reswitching, are two-fold. 1. Any tradeoff between present and future goods is subject to diminishing returns. . . . 2. The lower is the interest rate (or profit rate - they are the same thing in the absence of uncertainty) - the higher will be the real wage.[25]

Furthermore, Kaldor's technical progress function (see Chapter 13 of this book) may be regarded as an attempt to repudiate the importance of reswitching techniques, particularly within a spectrum, under a given state of technology.

---

[24]Paul A. Samuelson, "Parables and Realism in Capital Theory: The Surrogate Production Function," Review of Economic Studies, Vol. 39, 1962, pp. 193-206. In this well-known paper, Samuelson sets out to show that the neoclassical parables can be validated even in a world of fixed proportions and heterogeneous capital goods. The crucial assumption of his model is that the production functions for the capital and consumption goods are identically the same. In other words, he is invoking the so-called "many-products-one-technique" simplification. Mark Blaug observes: "It is ironic that the assumption of equal capital-labour ratios in all industries used by Samuelson to defend the concept of an aggregate production function validates the labour theory value and indeed Marx's labour theory of surplus value, although of course in these circumstances a capital theory of surplus value would do just as well." Mark Blaug, The Cambridge Revolution: Success or Failure (London: The Institute of Economic Affairs, 1975), p. 37 n.

[25]Paul A. Samuelson, Economics, 9th Edition, op. cit., p. 616.

And finally, in 1975, Joan Robinson, the initiator, also conceded that the reswitching phenomena was not crucial to the alternative paradigm in growth theory.[26]

References

Blaug, M., _Economic Theory in Retrospect_ (Homewood, Ill.: R.D. Irwin, 1968).

_____, _The Cambridge Revolution: Success or Failure_ (London: The Institute of Economic Affairs, 1975).

Bohm-Bawerk, E. v., _The Positive Theory of Capital_ (South Holland, Ill.: Libertarian Press, 1959).

Champernowne, D.G., "The Production Function and the Theory of Capital: A Comment," _Review of Economic Studies_, Vol. 21, 1953-4.

Harcourt, G.C., _Some Cambridge Controversies in the Theory of Capital_ (Cambridge: Cambridge University Press, 1972).

Kregel, J.A., _Rate of Profit, Distribution and Growth: Two Views_ (London: Macmillan, 1971).

_____, _The Reconstruction of Political Economy: An Introduction to Post-Keynesian Economics_ (New York: John Wiley & Sons, 1973).

Lutz, A., _The Theory of Interest_ (Chicago: Aldine Publishing Co., 1966).

Quarterly Journal of Economics, "Paradoxes in Capital Theory: A Symposium," _Quarterly Journal of Economics_, Vol. LXXX, November 1966.

Robinson, J., _Accumulation of Capital_ (London: Macmillan, 1956).

_____, _Collected Economic Papers_, Vol. 2 (Oxford: Blackwell, 1965).

_____, "The Unimportance of Reswitching," _Quarterly Journal of Economics_, 89, 1975.

[26] Joan Robinson, "The Unimportance of Reswitching," _Quarterly Journal of Economics_, 89 (1975): 32-39.

Rymes, T.K., On Concepts of Capital and Technical Change (London: Cambridge University Press, 1971).

Samuelson, P., Economics, 9th Edition (New York: McGraw-Hill, 1973).

_____, "Parables and Realism in Capital Theory: The Surrogate Production Function," Review of Economic Studies, Vol. 39, June 1962.

_____, "A Summing Up," Quarterly Journal of Economics, Vol. 80, November 1966.

Solow, R.M., Capital Theory and the Rate of Return (Chicago: Rand McNally & Co., 1965).

Sraffa, P., Production of Commodities By Means of Commodities (London: Cambridge University Press, 1960).

Swan, T.W., "Economic Growth and Capital Accumulation," Economic Record, Vol. 32, November 1956.

Uhr, C.G., "Wicksell, A Centennial Evaluation," American Economic Review, Vol. 41, December 1951.

Wicksell, K., Lectures on Political Economy (London: Routledge & Kegan Paul, Ltd., 1934).

_____, Value, Capital and Rent (New York: Rinehart, 1954).

Chapter 12

JOAN ROBINSON'S "HISTORICAL MODEL"

Joan Robinson originally set out to investigate the effects of distribution on capital accumulation. She discovered that in neither the Walrasian nor the Marshallian neoclassical system was there an explanation for the determination of the rate of profit. Similarly barren, contemporary economic theory does not provide a satisfactory answer to this problem. It may be initially puzzling to readers of her work that she should raise the question as to what determines the rate of profit.[1] For students of economics have always been taught that in equilibrium the rate of profit is determined by the marginal productivity of capital. Furthermore, general equilibrium theory has shown us that the equilibrium values of all variables in a model are simultaneously determined; there is no one-way -direction causal relation. Why then does Professor Robinson place the determination of the rate of profit at the very foundation of theoretical analysis? Her reasons may be stated as follows:

(a) Sraffa's analysis and the reswitching phenomena have demonstrated that it is impossible to derive the rate of profit by taking the marginal product of the homogeneous capital entering a production function. For the rate of profit must be known _first_ before the value of the homogeneous capital stock can be determined. Thus, Joan Robinson rejects the marginal productivity theory as highly circular and untenable.

---

[1] Joan Robinson, _Essays in the Theory of Economic Growth_ (New York: St. Martin's Press, 1962), pp. 10-11. She writes: "Technical conditions and the rate of profit determine the pattern of normal prices, including the price of labour-time in terms of each commodity; money-wage rates determine the corresponding money price level. But what determines the rate of profit? . . . Marshall conceals the problem behind a smoke-screen of moral sentiments. The latter-day neoclassicals are forever chasing definitions round a circular argument."

(b) Professor Robinson points out that the time through which general-equilibrium theory (neoclassical) moves is "logical" time, not "historical" time. She writes: "In a model depicting equilibrium positions there is no causation. It consists of a closed circle of simultaneous equations. The value of each element is entailed by the values of the rest. At any moment in logical time, the past is determined as much by the future."[2] On the other hand, she asserts: "In an historical model, causal relations have to be specified. Today is a break in time between an unknown future and an irrevocable past. What happens next will result from the interactions of the behaviour of human beings within the economy. Movement can only be forward."[3] Hence, causation is important to her.

(c) In the spirit of Ricardo, the direction of causation envisioned by Joan Robinson runs from the effect of the rate of profit on distribution then, in turn, to the effect of distribution on capital accumulation. Since she rejects the marginal productivity theory of distribution, Joan Robinson and other members of the Anglo-Italian school have to seek an explanation for the determination of the rate of profit from factors outside of the production system itself, such as the Keynesian analysis of saving and investment, the saving propensities of the social classes, and the Harrodian concept of warranted and natural growth rates of output. It is interesting to note that Keynes revived the Ricardian method of analysis.[4] Like Ricardo, Keynes emphasized causal determination in his theory. In this regard, the Hicksian IS-LM analysis is un-Keynesian. As pointed out by Luigi L. Pasinetti, "Hicks has in fact broken up Keynes' basic chain of arguments. The relations have been turned into a system of simultaneous equations, i.e.,

---

[2]Joan Robinson, Essays in the Theory of Economic Growth, p. 26.

[3]Ibid.

[4]This is the observation of Luigi L. Pasinetti. See his Growth and Income Distribution, op. cit., pp. 42-44.

precisely into what Keynes did not want them to be."[5]
This point is made clear by Keynes' attack on the neoclassical tenet which maintained that saving and investment are simultaneously determined by the rate of interest. Keynes, on the other hand, insisted that it is
investment that determines saving - a one-way-direction
relation.

The Robinsonian objective is to build a historical
(causal) model. She points out:

> To build a causal model, we must start not
> from equilibrium relations but from rules
> and motives governing human behaviour. We
> therefore have to specify to what kind of
> economy the model applies, for the various
> economies have different sets of rules.[6]

The historical model Joan Robinson outlined represents her initial attempt to analyze the growth process
of the modern capitalist world. The determinants of the
growth process are grouped by her under seven headings:
(1) Technical conditions; (2) investment policy; (3)
thriftiness conditions; (4) competitive conditions;
(5) the wage bargain; (6) financial conditions; and
(7) the initial stock of capital goods and the state of
expectations formed by past experience.[7]

---

[5]Luigi L. Pasinetti, op. cit., p. 46. This view is shared
by most of the critics of the IS-LM analysis. For instance,
Axel Leijonhufvud in his important book, On Keynesian Economics and the Economics of Keynes (New York: Oxford University Press, 1968) writes: "For the majority of economists, this standard income-expenditure model has reached
the same position of established orthodoxy as that occupied
in the interwar period by the Marshallian economics from
which Keynes had to wage such a hard 'struggle to escape.'"
(p. 4.) The main thesis of Leijonhufvud's book "is that
Keynes' theory is quite distinct from the 'Keynesian' income-expenditure theory." (p. 8.) In a similar vein, Joan
Robinson on various occasions also criticized the Hicks-
Hansen IS-LM apparatus. See her "The Second Crisis of
Economic Theory" in Papers and Proceedings of the American
Economic Association Annual Meeting, December 27-29, 1971.

[6]Joan Robinson, op. cit., p. 34.

[7]Ibid., pp. 35-45.

It should be noted that Joan Robinson's two books,
The Accumulation of Capital (1956) and Essays in the
Theory of Economic Growth (1962), together with N. Kaldor's
article, "Alternative Theories of Distribution" (1955-6),
mark the beginning of the alternative paradigm in growth
theory. Since then, a more comprehensive post-Keynesian
paradigm in economics has emerged of which analysis of
economic growth is only a component part.[8] What Joan
Robinson attempts to convey in the above-mentioned two
books is the idea that in the analysis of the growth
process one should discard the preoccupation with the
determination of mathematical properties of the model.
One should emphasize instead the qualitative change in
the growth process as reflected in her seven determinants.
In the light of the emerging post-Keynesian paradigm in
economics, the spirit of her intent is best summarized by
John Cornwall:

> In summary, post-Keynesian macrodynamics
> can be seen as an attempt to incorporate
> both the institutional framework of ad-
> vanced market economy and the manner in
> which this institutional framework changes
> over time into the explanation of growth
> and cyclical process. Unlike neoclassical
> macrodynamics, it strives to encompass the
> real world of uncertainty, oligopolies,
> new products and technologies, a world in
> which the "human element" is reflected in
> the quality of the entrepreneurial class.
> The view of post-Keynesian economists is
> that only by incorporating these elements
> into the analysis can macrodynamics even
> begin to suggest solutions to the problems
> of the real world.[9]

---

[8]See Alfred S. Eichner and J.A. Kregel, "An Essay on
Post-Keynesian Theory: A New Paradigm in Economics,"
op. cit.; and Alfred S. Eichner, "Post-Keynesian Theory:
An Introduction" and John Cornwall, "Post-Keynesian
Theory: Macrodynamics" in Challenge, Vol. 21, No. 2,
May/June 1978.

[9]John Cornwall, op. cit., p. 16.

The central mechanism of the Robinsonian historical model is the double-sided relationship between the rate of profit and the rate of capital accumulation. In addition, this is one of the essential elements in the emerging post-Keynesian economics. As pointed out by Alfred S. Eichner, post-Keynesian theory offers an explanation of the linkage between economic growth and income distribution; investment is the key determinant for both.[10] This double-sided relationship is explained by Joan Robinson as follows:

> The accumulation going on in a particular situation determines the level of profits obtainable in it, and thus (on the basis of the type of expectations which we have postulated) determines the rate of profit expected on investment. The rate of profit in turn influences the rate of accumulation. The rate of profit generated by a particular situation may be such as to induce a rate of accumulation greater or less than that which is actually taking place.[11]

The various possible relations between the rate of profit and capital accumulation are depicted by the following Robinsonian diagram:

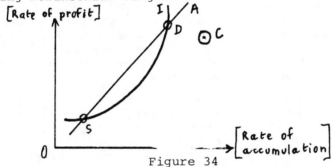

Figure 34

---

[10]Alfred S. Eichner, op. cit., p. 8. Eichner writes, "This follows from an underlying belief that in a dynamic, expanding economy (paraphrasing neoclassical terminology), the income effects produced by investment and other sources of growth far outweigh the substitution effects resulting from price movements. That is, changes in demand, both aggregate and sectoral, are due more to changes in income than to changes in relative prices. Indeed, the importance attached to income - as opposed to substitution - effects is the sensitive barometer of just how post-Keynesian, or even Keynesian, any particular piece of analysis is." op. cit., p. 8.

[11]Joan Robinson, op. cit., p. 47. The diagram is on p. 48.

The diagram is designed to show the "short-period situations which chances and changes of history throw up."[12]   The curve A represents the expected rate of profit on investment as a function of the rate of accumulation $(\frac{I}{K} \equiv \frac{\dot{K}}{K})$ that generates it.   It is the locus of all those possible expected rates of profit that justify the investment plans drawn up by firms, oligopolistic or otherwise.   Point C, which is to the right of curve A in Figure 34, indicates a situation in which the firms' investment plans and the rate of accumulation are higher than the justifiable rates of profit.   Consequently, the rate of accumulation will fall in the immediate future. On the other hand, when the current rate of accumulation is less than would be justified by the rate of profit that it is generating, the rate of accumulation will rise at the next round.   Such possible situations would be located within the area between D and S in Figure 34.

The desired rate of accumulation is indicated by point D in the diagram.   It is a situation in which firms' rates of accumulation generate just the expected rates of profit that are required to cause them to be maintained. If this position is maintained over time, "we now proceed to confront the desired rate of growth (resulting from the 'animal spirits' of the firms) with the rate of growth made possible by physical conditions (resulting from the growth of population and technical knowledge)."[13]   This situation is nicknamed by Joan Robinson as the "Golden Age" growth rate where lambent tranquility prevails and expectations are never disappointed.

However, Joan Robinson warns: "The fact that the desired and actual rates of accumulation coincide in a particular short-period situation does not by itself guarantee that they will continue to do so."[14]   For "uncertainty, through the volatility of expectations to which it gives rise, is continually leading the firms into self-contradictory policies. Now it needs no chance shocks to set an upswing going. The model is inherently unstable and fluctuates even in otherwise tranquil conditions."[15]   Although she did not develop an analysis of

---

[12]Joan Robinson, op. cit., p. 48.

[13]Ibid., p. 52.

[14]Ibid., p. 49.

[15]Ibid., p. 67.

short-period cyclical fluctuations, Professor Robinson certainly recognized the need to distinguish between the factors responsible for the long-run growth of output and those responsible for short-run fluctuations around the trend line. Even in the analysis of growth, she does not restrict herself to defining the necessary conditions for the "Golden Age" path. Various alternative possible growth paths have been suggested by her, such as: "Limping Golden Age," representing growth at less than full employment, "Leaden Age," describing growth with rising rates of unemployment, "Bastard Golden Age," and so on.[16]

Joan Robinson employs the "Golden Age" model to make comparisons between economies, each growing at a uniform but different rate. One of the objectives of this exercise is to provide a theoretical groundwork for the determinants of the rate of profit other than those given by the marginal productivity theory. For example, if firms in two "Golden Age" systems have the same "animal spirits" as reflected by the identical I-curves in Figures 35a and 35b, respectively, and if the average propensity to save is higher in Economy b than that in a, then the rate of profits and the rate of accumulation would be lower in Economy b than those in Economy a. The higher average propensity to save in b is depicted by the A-curve in Figure 35b lying lower than the A-curve in Figure 35a. Consequently, point D_b lies further to the left on the I-curve in Figure 35b.

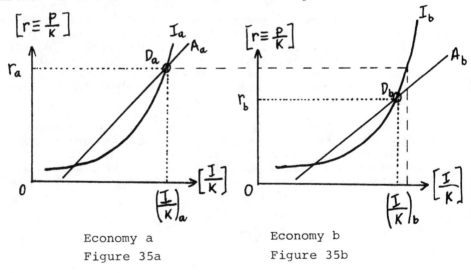

Economy a

Figure 35a

Economy b

Figure 35b

[16]Joan Robinson, op. cit., pp. 52-59.

It is clear that the equilibrium rate of profit r_a is higher than the equilibrium rate of profit r_b and that the equilibrium $\left(\frac{I}{K}\right)_a$ is also higher than the equilibrium $\left(\frac{I}{K}\right)_b$. Furthermore, both r_a and r_b are determined by two basic factors, namely the average propensity to save out of gross profit (using the Ricardo-von Neumann-Kalecki assumption that savings of workers are equal to zero) and the rate of capital accumulation, which in "Golden Age" conditions is equal to the rate of growth of the labor force. Symbolically, the equation for the determination of the rate of profit may be written as:

$$r \equiv \frac{P}{K} = \frac{1}{s_c} \frac{\dot{K}}{K} = \frac{n}{s_c}$$

where r is the rate of profit; P denotes profits; s_c stands for the average propensity to save out of gross profit; and n represents the Harrodian constant growth rate of the labor force.

In rejecting the marginal productivity theory, Joan Robinson found the determinants of the rate of profit outside of the production system. It is interesting to note that the inverse relation between r and s_c, implied by the equation for the rate of profit, is the application of Keynes' "paradox of thrift" in the long run. Thus, Joan Robinson writes: "When the actual rate of growth is limited only by the desired rate, therefore, greater thrift is associated with a low rate of accumulation. This is the central paradox of the General Theory projected into long-period analysis."[17]

The linkage between economic growth and income distribution through investment has also been demonstrated by the Robinsonian analysis. For once the rate of profit is determined, the income share of the capitalists in the national income is also determined.

------

[17] Joan Robinson, op. cit., p. 60.

In the views of Joan Robinson and other members of
the Anglo-Italian school, the savings ratio can be highly
variable in both the short and the long run. In fact,
changes in the savings ratio through changes in the distribution of income are regarded as the adjustment mechanism for correcting disequilibrium in the short run and
for bringing the actual growth rate in line with the
natural growth rate in the long run. This adjustment
mechanism is different from that of Keynes stated in The
General Theory. For Keynes suggested that changes in the
level of employment were the primary short-run adjustment
mechanism. However, Joan Robinson points out that there
may be limits to Keynes' suggestion. One of these is
what she calls the "inflation barrier." She writes:

> But there is a limit to the possible maxi-
> mum quasi-rent to wages, which is set by
> what we may call the inflation barrier.
> Higher prices of consumption goods rela-
> tively to money-wage rates involve a lower
> real consumption by workers. There is a
> limit to the level to which real-wage rates
> can fall without setting up a pressure to
> raise money-wage rates. But a rise in
> money-wage rates increases money expendi-
> ture, so that the vicious spiral of money-
> wages chasing prices sets in. There is
> then a head-on conflict between the desire
> of entrepreneurs to invest and the refusal
> of the system to accept the level of real
> wages which the investment entails; some-
> thing must give way. Either the system
> explodes in a hyper-inflation, or some[18]
> check operates to curtail investment.

The "inflation barrier" may be prevented by technical progress which increases real-wage rates by raising
output per man. Hence, an increased rate of capital accumulation will be permitted to take place.

In discussing technical progress, Joan Robinson makes
the distinction between (a) changes in the spectra of techniques available, and (b) changes in the choice of technique within a given spectrum at a point in time. It is

---

[18]Joan Robinson, The Accumulation of Capital, op. cit., p. 48.

in the second case that capital-reversing (Ruth Cohen's Curiosum) and capital reswitching occur. These problems raise the question of valuation of the existing capital stock that goes into the production function. This is the origin of her criticism of the neoclassical marginal productivity theory of distribution. In the spirit of Ricardo, Joan Robinson attempts to find an invariable measure of capital value independent of distribution. Like Ricardo, she also finds the problem exceedingly difficult to solve:

> Indeed, in reality it is insoluble in prin-
> ciple, for the composition of output, the
> characteristics of men employed and the
> techniques in use are all different in any
> two positions, and in any position the stock
> of capital goods in existence is not that
> which is appropriate to the conditions ob-
> taining in that position, but is made up of
> fossils representing the phases of develop-
> ment through which the economy has been pass-
> ing. The historical cost of existing equip-
> ment is out of gear with its value based on
> expected future earnings, and that value is
> clouded by the uncertainty that hangs over
> the future. Only the roughest kind of mea-
> surement can be made in actual cases.[19]

The "roughest kind of measurement" she suggests is the real-capital ratio. Following C.E. Ferguson's alge-braic interpretation,[20] the real-capital ratio is ob-tained in the following way: First, let us denote the value of capital in terms of commodities by K. Then, we divide K by the real-wage rate w. This procedure trans-forms the value of capital in terms of commodities into the value of capital in terms of labor time. Finally, we divide K/w by the amount of labor employed when the capital equipment is operating at normal capacity, the real-capital ratio, K/wL, is obtained. (Recall the labor theory of value.)

---

[19] Joan Robinson, op. cit., p. 117.

[20] C.E. Ferguson, The Neoclassical Theory of Production and Distribution, op. cit., p. 325. It is interesting to note that Ferguson, a staunch defender of neoclassical theory, criticizes Robinson's writings as mathematically intractable Therefore, in his algebraic formulation of the Robinson model, Ferguson has to employ some drastic simplifications and modifications.

Ferguson's algebraic formulation permits a more vigorous statement of the Robinsonian emphasis on the necessity and effect of the determination of the rate of profit on the distribution of income and economic growth:

$$(1) \quad Y = W + P = wL + rK$$

This is the equation for the distribution of income, which may be rewritten as

$$(2) \quad W = Y - P$$

$$(3) \quad \text{Let } k = \frac{K}{wL}$$

$$(4) \quad r = \frac{P}{K} = \left(\frac{W}{W}\right)\frac{P}{k} = \frac{P}{W}\frac{wL}{K} = \frac{P}{W}\frac{1}{k}$$

$$(5) \quad \frac{P}{W} = \frac{rK}{wL} = rk$$

$$(6) \quad P = rk(W) = rk(Y - P)$$

Equation (6) may be solved to show the relation among the profit share, P/Y, the rate of profit, r, and the real-capital ratio, k:

$$P = rkY - rkP$$

$$P(1 + rk) = rkY$$

$$\frac{P}{Y} = \frac{rk}{1 + rk}$$

$$(7) \quad \frac{P}{Y} = \frac{1}{1 + (1/rk)}$$

The positive relation between P/Y and r or k is clearly conveyed by equation (7). Lurking behind this equation are the seven determinants of the Robinsonian "historical" model mentioned earlier in this chapter.

References

Cornwall, J., "Post-Keynesian Theory: Macrodynamics," Challenge, Vol. 21, May/June 1978.

Eichner, A.S., and Kregel, J.A., "An Essay on Post-Keynesian Theory: A New Paradigm in Economics," Journal of Economic Literature, Vol. XIII, December 1975.

Eichner, A.S., "Post-Keynesian Theory: An Introduction," Challenge, Vol. 21, No. 2, May/June 1978.

Ferguson, C.E., The Neoclassical Theory of Production and Distribution

Leijonhufvud, A., On Keynesian Economics and the Economics of Keynes (New York: Oxford University Press, 1968).

Pasinetti, L.L., Growth and Income Distribution (London: Cambridge University Press, 1974).

Robinson, J., The Accumulation of Capital (London: Macmillan, 1956).

_____, Essays in the Theory of Economic Growth (New York: St. Martin's Press, 1962).

_____, "The Second Crisis of Economic Theory," Papers and Proceedings of American Economic Association Annual Meeting, December 1971.

Chapter 13

THEORY OF DISTRIBUTION AND GROWTH
OF KALDOR AND PASINETTI

The Anglo-Italian School is not monolithic in view
on every aspect of distribution and growth theory. In
several respects, which we will consider below, the
methodology of Nicholas Kaldor and Luigi L. Pasinetti
is quite different from that of Joan Robinson. For instance, while Robinson in her "historical" model prefers
to give imprecise and flexible statements about investment and technical progress, Kaldor and Pasinetti are
not wary about precise formulations of both subjects.
Further, on the question of measurement of capital,
Kaldor and Pasinetti also differ from Robinson. In his
technical progress function, Kaldor avoids using the
concept of capital stock. Instead, he uses the variable
rate of increase in gross investment. Thus, he is able
to extricate himself from the thorny "Ricardian problem"
of finding an invariable measure of value, independent of
distribution.

While Joan Robinson is troubled by capital-reversing
and reswitching in the choice of technique within a given
spectrum, Kaldor simply adopts the fixed pay-off period
criterion for investment decisions. In addition, on the
question of long-run steady-state growth, Joan Robinson
does not consider full employment at each point in time
as a necessary condition. Hence, she suggests various
alternative growth paths. Kaldor-Pasinetti, on the other
hand, argue that only full-employment equilibrium is constant with steady-state growth. The Kaldorian justification for assuming full employment at each point in time is
explained by using the device of a representative firm
as depicted by Figure 36.[1]

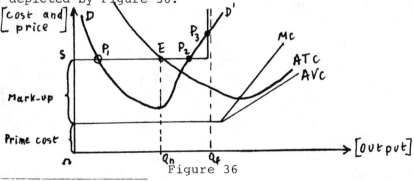

Figure 36

---

[1]See Nicholas Kaldor, "Economic Growth and the Problem of
Inflation," Economica, Vol. 26 (Aug.-Nov. 1959) and "Capital

The Kaldorian short-run representative firm pos-
sesses a certain degree of monopoly power (Kalecki's
influence). Therefore, it is able to set the level of
profit by a mark-up over prime costs, which are mainly
labor costs. The average variable (prime) cost curve
is constant up to the point of optimum capacity utilization. Constant AVC naturally implies constant marginal
cost. However, average total cost is shown to be still
falling after the inflection point of AVC. This is due
to the monotonically falling average fixed costs. Kaldor assumes that the primary constraint in the short run
is the availability of labor. Accordingly, the supply
curve, SS', is in the form of a reversed letter L. Because once the full-employment output level Q_f is ap-
proached, SS' becomes perpendicular.

Turning now to the U-shaped demand curve DD', Kaldor
assumes that the demand for consumption goods produced by
the firm is linked to the distribution of income. Given
the historically determined constant money-wage rate,
the higher the supply price relative to the prime cost,
the greater the profit share. As the wage share de-
clines, however, the demand for consumption goods also
falls - and vice versa. Hence, the slope of the demand
curve is negative up to the point where ATC intersects
SS'. Once that point is passed, ATC lies below SS' and
the profit share rises. Consequently, induced investment takes place and the slope of DD' turns upward.[2]

Accumulation and Economic Growth," in F.A. Lutz and D.C.
Hague, eds., The Theory of Capital, International Economic
Association, Corfu Conference (London: Macmillan, 1961).

[2]Henry Y. Wan, Jr., in his Economic Growth (New York:
Harcourt Brace Jovanovich, 1971), pp. 85-87, gives an
algebraic formulation of the Kaldorian DD' as follows:

(1) $\quad \dfrac{P}{Y} = \dfrac{rK}{Y} = \left(\dfrac{1}{s_c - s_w}\right)\dfrac{I}{Y} - \left(\dfrac{s_w}{s_c - s_w}\right)$

This is Kaldor's profit share equation, the derivation of
which will be taken up in the following pages of this
chapter. The symbols s_c and s_w stand for saving ratios
out of profit and wage shares, respectively.

(2) $\quad \dfrac{P}{Y} = \dfrac{P_d - ATC}{P_d} = 1 - \dfrac{ATC}{P_d}$

where P_d is the Marshallian demand price. Substituting
(1) into (2) and rearranging terms:

154

The U-shaped demand curve intersects SS' at three points. P_1 is a stable, under-employment equilibrium point which is not considered by Kaldor as compatible with steady-state growth. P_2 is an unstable equilibrium situation which is also rejected in the Kaldorian growth theory. Only P_3 is considered to be compatible with long-run steady-state growth for it is a stable full-employment equilibrium point. Such is Kaldor's justification for assuming full employment.

In the following sections we shall discuss three models which study the relation between distribution and growth. We will address Kaldor's "widow's cruse" theory of distribution first. Then, Pasinetti's re-formulation of Kaldor's distribution theory will be explained. And finally, the Kaldor-Mirrlees growth model with endogenous technical progress will be considered.

Kaldor's "Widow's Cruse" Theory of Distribution[3]

Like Robinson, Kaldor makes investment the key determinant in his theory of distribution and growth. In his "widow's cruse" model, Kaldor assumes a state of full employment so that total output or income is given.

$$(3) \quad \frac{ATC}{P_d} = 1 - \frac{P}{Y} = 1 - \left[\left(\frac{1}{s_c - s_w} \right) \frac{I}{Y} - \left(\frac{s_w}{s_c - s_w} \right) \right]$$

$$(4) \quad \frac{ATC}{P_d} = \frac{s_c - \frac{I}{Y}}{s_c - s_w}$$

$$(5) \quad ATC(s_c - s_w) = (s_c - \frac{I}{Y}) P_d$$

$$(6) \quad P_d = \frac{(s_c - s_w) \, ATC}{s_c - \frac{I}{Y}}$$

Equation (6) shows that when the I/Y ratio rises, P_d also rises. This is the explanation for the upward sloping of DD'.

[3]Nicholas Kaldor, "Alternative Theories of Distribution," originally published in the Review of Economic Studies, Vol. 23, No. 2, 1955-56, reprinted in Kaldor's Essays on Value and Distribution (Illinois: The Free Press of Glencoe, 1969), pp. 209-236.

Writing S_w and S_c for aggregate savings out of wages and profits, Kaldor formulates the following income identities:

  (1) $Y = W + P$, where W stands for wage-earners'
              income and P represents capital-
              ists' income.

  (2) $I = S$.

  (3) $S = S_w + S_c$

     "The interpretative value of the model," Kaldor writes, "depends on the 'Keynesian' hypothesis that investment, or rather, the ratio of investment to output, can be treated as an independent variable, invariant with respect to changes in the two savings propensities."[4] Treating investment as an exogenous variable and assuming simple proportional savings functions:

  (4) $S_w = s_w W$

  (5) $S_c = s_c P$

Kaldor obtains:

  (6) $I = s_c P + s_w W = s_c P + s_w (Y - P) = (s_c - s_w) P + s_w Y$

Dividing equation (6) by Y, the equation for the profit share in income is derived:

  (7) $\dfrac{P}{Y} = -\left(\dfrac{s_w}{s_c - s_w}\right) + \left(\dfrac{1}{s_c - s_w}\right)\dfrac{I}{Y}$

Then, the equation for the rate of profit is obtained by dividing equation (6) by K:

  (8) $r = \dfrac{P}{K} = -\left(\dfrac{s_w}{s_c - s_w}\right)\dfrac{Y}{K} + \left(\dfrac{1}{s_c - s_w}\right)\dfrac{I}{K}$

---

[4]Nicholas Kaldor, op. cit., p. 229.

Now, equation (7) states that, given the wage-earners' and capitalists' propensities to save, the share of profit in income depends on the ratio of investment to output.[5] This proposition is described graphically by Figure 37:

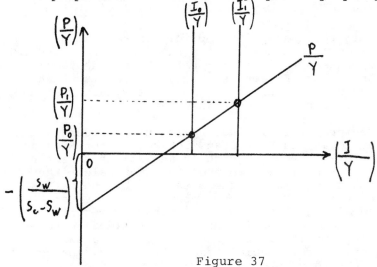

Figure 37

Given the exogenously determined $\frac{I_\circ}{Y}$, the share of profit will be $\frac{P}{Y}$. If the ratio of investment to output is higher, say $\frac{I_1}{Y}$, then the share of profit will also be higher: $\left(\frac{P_1}{Y}\right)$.

The stability condition for the model is:

$$(9) \quad s_c > s_w .$$

For, under the assumption of full employment, when ex ante investment is greater than ex ante savings, an inflationary gap will appear in the output market. Consequently, profit margins will also rise. If $s_c > s_w$, this redistribution of income in favor of profits will increase aggregate real saving. This adjustment mechanism through a flexible saving ratio will ensure the homeostasis of equality between planned investment. In the converse case as well, the flexible saving ratio will serve as the equilibrating mechanism.

---

[5]This is Ferguson's diagram. See C.E. Ferguson, _op. cit._, p. 315.

Kaldor points out that in the limiting case where $S_w = 0$, equation (7) can be rewritten as:

$$(10) \quad \frac{P}{Y} = \frac{1}{S_c} \frac{I}{Y}$$

"This is the assumption implicit in Keynes' parable about the widow's cruse - where a rise in entrepreneurial consumption raises their total profit by an identical amount - and of Mr. Kalecki's theory of profits which can be paraphrased by saying that 'capitalists earn what they spend, and workers spend what they earn.'"[6]

Furthermore, this is what Pasinetti considers as the "new answer to an old Ricardian problem." "For Ricardo the wage-rate is fixed exogenously and all that remains (after paying rents) goes to profits. For Kaldor the rate of profit is determined exogenously by the natural rate of growth and capitalists' propensity to save; and all that remains goes to wages. For the former it is profits that take up the features of a residual category; for the latter it is wages."[7] Kaldor's "new answer" is most explicit in the special case. If $s_w = 0$, the equation for the rate of profit is transformed into:

$$(11) \quad r = \frac{P}{K} = \frac{1}{S_c} \frac{I}{K} = \frac{1}{S_c} \frac{\dot{K}}{K}$$

In a state of continuous full employment, Harrod's "natural rate of growth" will prevail. It will be recalled that the condition for Harrod's Gn abstracted from technical progress is $s = \beta n$. Substituting this condition $\left(\frac{\dot{K}}{K} = \frac{s}{\beta} = n\right)$ into equation (11), one obtains:

$$(12) \quad r = \frac{P}{K} = \frac{n}{S_c}$$

After stating the "widow's cruse theory of distribution, Kaldor proceeds to show the linkage between distribution and growth through the key determinant, investment. Following Harrod, Kaldor first attempts to show the relation between I/Y and Harrod's warranted growth rate, Gw. This is accomplished through the acceleration principle:

---

[6] N. Kaldor, op. cit., p. 230.

[7] Luigi L. Pasinetti, op. cit., pp. 101-102.

(13) $\quad I = \beta \, \Delta Y$

Dividing equation (13) by Y, one obtains:

(14) $\quad \dfrac{I}{Y} = \beta \, \dfrac{\Delta Y}{Y} = \beta \, G_w$

Rearranging terms and substituting the equilibrium condition I = S ex ante into equation (14), one has:

(15) $\quad G_w = \dfrac{\frac{I}{Y}}{\beta} = \dfrac{\frac{S}{Y}}{\beta} = \dfrac{s_w + (s_c - s_w)\frac{P}{Y}}{\beta} \gtreqless G_n$

Kaldor points out: "The 'warranted' and the 'natural' rates of growth are not independent of one another; if profit margins are flexible, the former will adjust itself to the latter through a consequential change in P/Y."[8] What causes P/Y to change? The answer is, of course, given by equation (7).

However, Kaldor points out that there are limits to this equilibrating mechanism: (a) The first is that the real wage cannot fall below a certain minimum; (b) "the second is that the indicated share of profits cannot be below the level which yields the minimum rate of profit necessary to induce capitalists to invest their capital."[9] These constraints may be illustrated by Figure 38.[10]

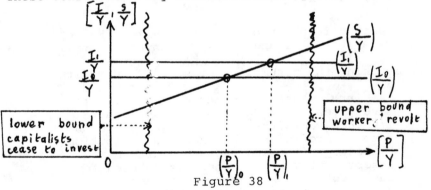

Figure 38

[8] N. Kaldor, op. cit., p. 232.

[9] Ibid., p. 233.

[10] This is Kaldor's diagram adopted by Harcourt with slight modifications. See G.C. Harcourt, Some Cambridge Controversies, op. cit., p. 209.

Pasinetti's Reformulation[11]

Pasinetti adds a new identity to the Kaldorian model:

(16) $\quad P = P_w + P_c$

where P_w and P_c stand for profits which accrue to the capitalists and profits which accrue to the workers. Consequently, the Kaldorian identity equations are revised as follows:

(17) $\quad Y = (W + P_w) + P_c$

(18) $\quad S = S_w + S_c$

The saving functions now become:

(19) $\quad S_w = s_w(W + P_w)$, and

(20) $\quad S_c = s_c P_c$

Thus, the equilibrium condition becomes:

(21) $\quad I = s_w(W + P_w) + s_c P_c = s_w Y + (s_c - s_w)P_c$

Pasinetti then proceeds to show that Kaldor's special case $(\frac{P}{Y} = \frac{1}{s_c} \frac{I}{Y}$ and $\frac{P}{K} = \frac{1}{s_c K})$ can be generalized without invoking the assumption of $s_w = 0$. He writes:

> The irrelevance of workers' propensity to save gives the model a much wider generality than was hitherto believed. Since the rate of profit and the income distribution between profits and wages are determined independently of s_w, there is no need for any hypothesis whatever on the aggregate savings behaviour of the workers.[12]

---

[11] Luigi L. Pasinetti, "Rate of Profit and Income Distribution in Relation to the Rate of Economic Growth," The Review of Economic Studies, Vol. 29, No. 4, October 1962, pp. 267-79, reprinted in Pasinetti, Growth and Income Distribution, op. cit.

[12] Ibid., p. 112.

The logic behind this paradoxical result may be stated in the following way: First, Pasinetti takes advantage of some of the standard features of "Golden Age" growth. One of these is the proposition that along the "Golden Age" growth path the rates of growth of both the workers' capital stock and that of the capitalists must be equal to the growth rate of the labor force:

$$(22) \quad \frac{\dot{K}}{K} = \frac{\dot{K}_c}{K_c} = \frac{\dot{K}_w}{K_w} = \frac{\dot{L}}{L} = n$$

A second one of the standard features is the theorem that along the "Golden Age" growth path, there will be uniform rate of profit:

$$(23) \quad r = \frac{P}{K} = \frac{P_c}{K_c} = \frac{P_w}{K_w}$$

Next, Pasinetti introduces the "institutional principle." He writes: "The model has been built on the institutional principle, inherent in any production system, that wages are distributed among members of society in proportion to the amount of labour they contribute and profits are distributed in proportion to the amount of capital they own. The latter proposition implies something which has passed unnoticed so far, namely that, in the long run, profits will turn out to be distributed in proportion to the amount of savings which are contributed."[13] Thus, Pasinetti suggests the following relation:

$$(24) \quad \frac{P_c}{S_c} = \frac{P_w}{S_w}$$

Now, Pasinetti can proceed to derive his paradoxical result.[14] Equation (22) may be rewritten as:

$$(25) \quad \frac{\dot{K}_c}{K_c} - \frac{\dot{K}}{K} = 0$$

Since in equilibrium $I_c = \dot{K}_c = S_c = s_c P_c$, equation (25) can be transformed into:

---

[13]Luigi L. Pasinetti, op. cit., p. 110.

[14]The derivation in this section relies heavily on Daniel Hamberg's exposition in his Models of Economic Growth (New York: Harper & Row, 1971), pp. 98-99.

(26) $\dfrac{s_c P_c}{K_c} - \dfrac{I}{K} = 0$

Utilizing equation (23), equation (26) now becomes:

(27) $\dfrac{s_c P}{K} - \dfrac{I}{K} = 0$

Factoring out $\dfrac{1}{K}$, one obtains:

(28) $\dfrac{1}{K}[s_c P - I] = 0$

To satisfy equation (28), $s_c P$ must equal I. Re-writing this equality:

(29) $P = \dfrac{1}{s_c} I$

Dividing both sides of equation (29) by Y, Kaldor's equation for the share of profits is derived:

(30) $\dfrac{P}{Y} = \dfrac{1}{s_c} \dfrac{I}{Y}$

Dividing both sides of equation (29) by K, one obtains the Kaldorian equation for the rate of profit:

(31) $\dfrac{P}{K} = \dfrac{1}{s_c} \dfrac{I}{K} = \dfrac{n}{s_c}$

As a further proof of the proposition that $s_w W$ has no effect on the value of P/Y or P/K along the "Golden Age" growth path, one can rewrite Pasinetti's equation (24) as:

(32) $\dfrac{P_c}{s_c P_c} = \dfrac{P_w}{s_w(W + P_w)} \qquad \left[= \dfrac{P_c}{s_c} = \dfrac{P_w}{s_w}\right]$

Rearranging terms, one can transform equation (32) into:

(33) $s_w W = (s_c - s_w)P_w$

"These conclusions," writes Pasinetti, "now suddenly shed new light on the old classical idea, hinted at already at the beginning, of a relation between the savings of that group of individuals who are in the position to carry on the process of production and the process of accumulation."[15] He continues: "The novelty of the present analysis has been to show that the relation is valid independently of any of those assumptions. It is valid whatever the saving behaviour of the workers may be."[16]

What is the practical implication of the model? The answer is, according to Pasinetti, that, in order to maintain full employment over time, the amount of investment undertaken should be that which is required by technical progress and population growth. "And if this investment is carried out, the rate of profit (when uniformly applied) must be equal to the natural rate of growth."[17]

The case of a socialist system is most straightforward in this respect. In a socialist society, there are no capitalists. All savings are undertaken by the state. This means that the parameter s_c becomes unity ($s_c = 1$). Consequently, equations (30) and (31) are transformed into:

$$(34) \quad \frac{P}{Y} = \frac{I}{Y} \quad \text{and}$$

$$(35) \quad \frac{P}{K} = \frac{I}{K}$$

"with the evident meaning that, in equilibrium, total profits are equal to total investments, and the rate of profit (and of interest) is equal to the ratio of investment to capital, i.e., equal to the natural rate of growth."[18]

---

[15] Luigi L. Pasinetti, op. cit., p. 113.

[16] Ibid.

[17] Ibid., p. 119.

[18] Ibid., p. 117.

The Kaldor-Mirrlees Model[19]

The difference between Joan Robinson's methodology
and that of Kaldor is brought out in sharp relief by the
Kaldor-Mirrlees "putty-clay" model. While Robinson
places the determinant of the rate of profit at the base
of her analytical structure, the center piece of the
Kaldor-Mirrlees model is the revised technical progress
function.[20] For it is the deu ex machina which, in
collaboration with the given growth rate of the labor
force, determines the steady-state growth rates of all
relevant variables of the model.

The Kaldor-Mirrlees treatment of the technical progress function is based on (a) the putty-clay vintage
approach and (b) the concept of technical progress as a
learning process.

It should be noted that not only do important differences exist between the Kaldorian approach and that
of Robinson, but also that they exist between the present model and the Solow model, discussed in Chapter 6
of this book. In the first place, even though Solow

---

[19]Nicholas Kaldor and James A. Mirrlees, "A New Model of
Economic Growth," reprinted from the Review of Economic
Studies, Vol. 29 (June 1962), pp. 174-192 in Harold R.
Williams and John D. Huffnagle, eds., Macroeconomic Theory:
Selected Readings (New York: Appleton-Century-Crofts,
1969), pp. 504-527.

[20]The original function was stated in Kaldor's article,
"A Model of Economic Growth," reprinted from the Economic
Journal, Dec., 1957 in Nicholas Kaldor, Essays on Economic
Stability and Growth (Illinois: The Free Press of Glencoe,
1960), pp. 258-300. In rejecting the neoclassical production function, Kaldor writes: "It follows that a sharp or
clear-cut distinction between the movement along a 'production function' with a given state of knowledge, and a shift
in the 'production function' caused by a change in the state
of knowledge, is arbitrary and artificial. Hence instead of
assuming that some given rate of increase in productivity is
attributable to technical progress which is superimposed, so
to speak, on the growth of productivity attributable to capital accumulation, we shall postulate a single relationship
between the growth of capital and the growth of productivity
which incorporates the influence of both factors." Ibid., p.
265. In other words, Kaldor assumes a relation between the
rates of growth of output per man and capital per man:
$$\frac{1}{y}\frac{dy}{dt} = F\left(\frac{1}{k}\frac{dk}{dt}\right).$$

treats investment as the transmission mechanism for
technical progress, the source of technical progress
remains exogenous to his model. This is not the case
in the present model. Kaldor and Mirrlees' embodied
technical progress is endogenous. For they have taken
into consideration - in addition to the exogenous increase in technical knowledge - the notion that technical
progress is also partly the result of a learning process
on the part of entrepreneurs. In the words of Hahn and
Matthews, "The entrepreneur is seen as perpetually grop-
ing in a mist of uncertainty, gradually and imperfectly
learning his way on the basis of experience accruing to
him."[21] This notion is implied in the Kaldor-Mirrlees
revised technical progress function which relates the
annual rate of growth of productivity per worker operating on new machines to the rate of growth of gross investment per worker. For more investment provides not
only the opportunity for thorough exploration of the
existing technical knowledge, but also the impetus for
faster technical advances.

Secondly, although both models assume that all machines are of infinite durability in physical terms, in
the Solow model the question of obsolescence does not
arise; machines need never be scrapped. For there is
smooth substitution between machines and labor at all
times; and competition will see to it that less labor
will be allocated to machines of older vintages than to
new machines. "In this case," observes R.G.D. Allen,
"machines (like old soldiers) never die but simply fade
away."[22] Conversely, in the Kaldor-Mirrlees model, the
question of obsolescence has to be taken into consideration. Since factor substitution is impossible ex post,
labor will not be released from old machines to help man
the machines of the latest vintage. The solution is,
therefore, to scrap some old machines. Thus, the
economic life of a machine of given vintage becomes an
additional endogenous variable to be determined. The

---

[21]F.H. Hahn and R.C.O. Matthews, "The Theory of Economic
Growth: A Survey," in Surveys of Economic Theory, Vol.
II, prepared for the American Economic Association and
the Royal Economic Society (New York: St. Martin's Press,
1965), p. 67.

[22]R.G.D. Allen, Macroeconomic Theory (New York: St.
Martin's Press, 1967), p. 283.

criterion for scrapping the machine as obsolescent is
its quasi-rent. Along the steady-state growth path,
the real-wage rate rises and the quasi-rents of old
machines continue to decline and eventually, become
zero. Hence, an additional equilibrium condition
emerges, i.e., the obsolescence condition of zero quasi-
rent. Here again, the model has an obvious affinity to
the Ricardian theory of rent. The no-rent machine corresponds to Ricardo's no-rent land and the condition of
obsolescence becomes the extensive margin of the Kaldor-
Mirrlees model.

Third, Kaldor and Mirrlees give more emphasis on
uncertainty and expectations about the future than Solow
does in his 1960 model. This point is highlighted by
their investment function. Under conditions of continuous technical progress, expectations concerning the
future are uncertain and hazardous. "Hence, investment
projects which qualify for adoption must pass a further
test - apart from the test of earning a satisfactory rate
of profit - and that is that the cost of the fixed assets
must be 'recovered' within a certain period - i.e., that
the gross profit earned in the first h years of the operation must be sufficient to repay the cost of investment."[23]
In other words, Kaldor and Mirrlees invoke the simple
"rule of thumb" fixed pay-off period criterion for investment decisions. Solow does not employ this "rule of thumb"
in his 1960 model, nor does Joan Robinson in her analysis.
She is always very wary about any rigorous formulation of
an investment function.

The main thrust of the Kaldor-Mirrlees model is to
show that the "Golden Age" solution is possible if approp-
riate assumptions are made about its functional relationships. The following is a simplified version of the model.

(1) $S_t = s_c P_{ct}$

Equation (1) is the classical saving function assumed by
the architects of the model. They explain: "Savings out
of wages are ignored - i.e., that they are assumed to be
balanced by non-business (personal) investment (i.e., resi-
dential construction). The assumption that business savings

---

[23]Nicholas Kaldor and James A. Mirrlees, op. cit., p. 510.

are a constant proportion of gross profits (after tax) is well supported by data relating to gross corporate savings."[24] This savings assumption naturally leads to the "widow's cruse" theory of distribution. Hence, we have the following equation:

$$(2) \quad \frac{P_t}{Y_t} = \frac{1}{s} \frac{I_t}{Y_t}$$

As for any vintage model, we need two time variables: one for time denoted by t in the usual sense and the other Υ for the dating of vintage machines in use at time t.

$$(3) \quad L_t = L_0 e^{nt} \quad \text{and} \quad (3') \quad L_t = \int_{t-T}^{t} L\Upsilon \, d\Upsilon$$

Equation (3) is the assumption about the growth of the labor force which is the same as that of Harrod; equation (3') defines the aggregate of labor.

$$(4) \quad \frac{1}{q_t} \frac{dq_t}{dt} = F\left(\frac{1}{i_t} \frac{di_t}{dt} \right)$$

This is the technical progress function. $\frac{1}{q_t} \frac{dq_t}{dt}$ stands

for the annual rate of growth of productivity per worker operating on new machines; and $\frac{1}{i_t} \frac{di_t}{dt}$ denotes the rate

of growth of gross investment per worker.

$$(5) \quad \dot{i}_t = hq_t - \int_{t}^{t+h} w_x dx$$

Equation (5) is the investment function. The fixed pay-off period set in advance is indicated by the symbol h; the symbol x is a running time variable for integration from t to t + h; q_t stands for output per worker produced

by the new machine; and w represents the real-wage rate. If we write p_t for profit per worker, the initial level of

profit per worker from the new machine may be defined as: $p_t = q_t - w$. Equation (5) is in per capita terms. The total function is: $I_t = hQ_t - L_t \int_{t}^{t+h} w_x dx$.

---

[24] Nicholas Kaldor and James A. Mirrlees, op. cit., p. 511 n.

(6) $\quad Q_{t-T} - wL_{t-T} = 0$ and (6') $q_{t-T} = w$

Equation (6) is the condition for obsolescence; equation
(6') is the same condition stated in per capita terms.
The symbol T stands for the economic life of a machine of
given vintage. The subscript t-T has the same meaning as
the subscript τ.

    The "Golden Age" solution of the model depends upon
the well-behaved technical progress function. Figure 39
depicts the "Golden Age" growth path of the model.

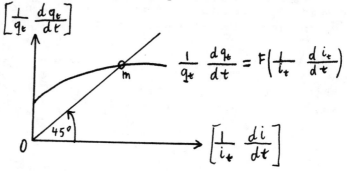

$$\frac{1}{q_t}\frac{dq_t}{dt} = F\left(\frac{1}{i_t}\frac{di_t}{dt}\right)$$

Figure 39

    The "Golden Age" growth path is indicated by the
point m at which the technical progress function intersects the 45 degree line. It should be noted that the
function is non-linear, showing the tendency towards
diminishing returns. However, this is not the same as
diminishing marginal productivity of capital: it merely
indicates that there is a certain limit to the learning
process. At the point m, there is a unique common value:

$$(7) \quad m = \frac{1}{q_t}\frac{dq_t}{dt} = \frac{1}{i_t}\frac{di}{dt} = \frac{1}{y_t}\frac{dy_t}{dt} = \frac{1}{w}\frac{dw}{dt}$$

    Since the aggregate output per man is defined as:
$y_t \equiv \frac{Y_t}{Lt}$, its "Golden Age" growth rate can be written as:

$$(8) \quad \frac{1}{y_t}\frac{dy_t}{dt} = \frac{1}{Y_t}\frac{dY_t}{dt} - n = m$$

    It follows that along the "Golden Age" growth path,
aggregate output will grow at the rate of m + n:

168

(9) $\dfrac{1}{Y_t} \dfrac{dY_t}{dt} = m + n$

where $Y_t = \displaystyle\int_{t-T}^{t} Q_\tau \, d\tau = \int_{\tau}^{t} q_\tau L_\tau d\tau$.

By the same reasoning, the "Golden Age" growth rates for gross investment per man and aggregate gross investment respectively are:

(10) $\dfrac{1}{i_t} \dfrac{di}{dt} = \dfrac{1}{I_t} \dfrac{dI_t}{dt} - n = m$ and

(11) $\dfrac{1}{I_t} \dfrac{dI_t}{dt} = m + n.$

The real-wage rate along the "Golden Age" growth path will also grow at the same rate of m; whereas the distribution of income, the rate of profit, and the economic life of machine (T), will remain constant over time.[25]

---

[25]Following R.G.D. Allen, the "Golden Age" growth rate for the real-wage rate may be derived as follows: Equation (6) can be rewritten as:

(a) $w = \dfrac{Q_{t-T}}{L_{t-T}} = q_{t-T} = q_t e^{-mT}$ where m and T are constant.

Taking the natural log of $w = q_t e^{-mT}$ in (a), we find $\ln w = \ln(q_t e^{-mT}) = \ln q_t + \ln e^{-mT} = \ln q_t - mT.$ Now differentiating this equation with respect to time, yields $\dfrac{d}{dt} \ln w = \dfrac{d}{dt} \ln q_t - \dfrac{d}{dt} mT.$ Since mT is constant, its time derivative is zero, thus $\dfrac{1}{w} \cdot \dfrac{dw}{dt} = \dfrac{1}{q_t} \cdot \dfrac{dq_t}{dt}.$ But we know that in the steady-state, q_t grows at the constant rate m, therefore

(b) $\dfrac{1}{w} \cdot \dfrac{dw}{dt} = \dfrac{1}{q_t} \cdot \dfrac{dq_t}{dt} = m$

which says that in the "Golden Age"," the real-wage rate grows at the constant rate m.

The constant T consistent with the "Golden Age" is derived by Allen in the following way: Rewriting equation (a) as:

169

These results appear to be very similar to those deduced from the corresponding neoclassical growth models. This is not surprising for both approaches are describing the characteristics of the "Golden Age" growth path. However, the tools employed in their respective analysis are quite different. In the words of Kaldor and Mirrlees:

> The model is Keynesian in its mode of operation (entrepreneurial expenditure decisions are primary, incomes, etc., are secondary) and severely non-neo-classical in that technological factors (marginal productivities or marginal substitution ratios) play no role in the determination of wages and profits. A "production function" in the sense of a single-valued relationship between some measure of capital, K_t, the labor force N_t, and of output Y_t (all at time t) clearly does not exist. Everything depends on past history, on how the collection of equipment goods which comprises K has been built up.[26]

(c) $e^{-mT} = w/q_t$ = constant, since w and q_t grow at the same rate m. So the consistent T is:

(d) $T = \frac{1}{m} \log \left(\frac{q_t}{w} \right)$

See R.G.D. Allen, op. cit., pp. 314-315.

[26] Nicholas Kaldor and James A. Mirrlees, op. cit., p. 522.

References

Allen, R.G.D., Macroeconomic Theory (New York: St. Martin's Press, 1967).

Ferguson, C.E., The Neoclassical Theory of Production and Distribution (Cambridge: Cambridge University Press, 1969).

Hahn, F.H., and Matthews, R.C.O., "The Theory of
    Economic Growth: A Survey," Economic Journal,
    Vol. 74, December 1974.

Hamberg, D., Models of Economic Growth (New York:
    Harper & Row, 1971).

Harcourt, G.C., Some Cambridge Controversies in the
    Theory of Capital (Cambridge: Cambridge Uni-
    versity Press, 1972).

Kaldor, N., "Economic Growth and the Problem of Infla-
    tion," Economica, Vol. 26, Aug.-Nov. 1959.

_____, Essays on Economic Stability and Growth
    (Illinois: The Free Press of Glencoe, 1960).

_____, Essays on Value and Distribution (Illinois:
    The Free Press of Glencoe, 1960).

_____, and Mirrlees, J.A., "A New Model of
    Economic Growth," Review of Economic Studies,
    Vol. 29, June 1962.

Lutz, F.A., and Hague, D.C., eds., The Theory of
    Capital (London: Macmillan, 1961).

Pasinetti, L., Growth and Income Distribution (London:
    Cambridge University Press, 1974).

Wan, H.Y., Economic Growth (New York: Harcourt Brace
    Jovanovich , 1971).

Chapter 14

EVALUATION OF THE TWO ALTERNATIVE APPROACHES

The Robinsonian and Kaldorian models considered in the preceding two chapters may be viewed as the vanguards of the emerging post-Keynesian theory. Although members of the Anglo-Italian School have succeeded in shaking the economic establishment from their complacency, they have also left a number of theoretical gaps which the current post-Keynesian writers are attempting to fill. "At this stage in its development," candidly states Alfred S. Eichner, "post-Keynesian theory remains far from a settled orthodoxy."[1]

The strongest point of the Robinsonian and Kaldorian analyses is their emphasis on the historical and institutional content of distribution theory to which mainstream writers have not given sufficient attention. In the witty words of William J. Baumol, "A distribution theory which ignores such fundamental relationships is, indeed, a performance of Hamlet in which the Prince of Denmark does not appear."[2] This point is important especially in policy implications. For Joan Robinson and other members of the Anglo-Italian School have shown the way to the current post-Keynesian writers to rethink the conventional wisdom in stabilization policy.[3]

---

[1] Alfred S. Eichner, "Post-Keynesian Theory: An Introduction," op. cit., p. 6.

[2] William J. Baumol, Economic Theory and Operations Analysis, 4th edition (Englewood Cliffs, N.J.: Prentice Hall, 1977), p. 699.

[3] Alfred S. Eichner writes: "If there is perhaps one point on which economists with a post-Keynesian perspective are likely to agree, it is that inflation cannot be controlled through conventional instruments of fiscal and monetary policy. It is because they regard inflation as resulting, not necessarily from any 'excess demand' for goods, but rather from a more fundamental conflict over the distribution of available income and ouput. The conventional policy instruments, by curtailing the level of economic activity, simply reduce the amount of income and output available for distribution, therefore heightening the social conflict underlying the inflationary process." op. cit., p. 10.

As to the issue of independency of investment which is considered by J.A. Kregel as the primary disagreement between the two approaches,[4] it is perhaps not of overriding importance. For this question depends upon the state of employment: If there is unemployment in existence, the "paradox of thrift" will be true; moreover, if full employment can be sustained, then saving determines investment. This issue was clarified by Keynes himself in the following words: "But if our central controls succeed in establishing an aggregate volume of output corresponding to full employment as nearly as is practicable, the classical theory comes into its own again from this point onwards."[5]

The most important theoretical gaps left by the pioneering models may be grouped under two main headings: (a) monetary analysis and (b) microeconomics. We shall first take up the gap in monetary analysis.

Both Robinson and Kaldor gave uncertainty and expectations much more emphasis than the architects of the "neoclassical synthesis" did. They also fully grasped the monetary perspective of J.M. Keynes. Nonetheless, "Ironically it was the real sector analysis of Kalecki that became the basis for further work at Cambridge," observes Alfred S. Eichner, "while Keynes' monetary perspective would be sustained elsewhere - by Shackle in Great Britain and by Sidney Weintraub, Paul Davidson, and Hyman P. Minsky in the United States."[6] This irony was inadvertently created by the Robinsonian and Kaldorian "Golden Age" analyses. Along the "Golden Age" growth path, tranquility prevails and uncertainty is absent.

---

[4] J.A. Kregel writes: "The important difference is in the assumption about investment. If savings determine investment then one is in the neoclassical pre-Keynesian world which produces the confusion between hard productive objects and finance as a logical necessity. The assumption of perfect foresight is simply another way of saying the same thing. Neoclassical theory is simply devoid of a theory of investment." Two Views, op. cit., p. 197.

[5] John Maynard Keynes, The General Theory of Employment Interest and Money, 1951 reprint (London: Macmillan), p. 378.

[6] Alfred S. Eichner, op. cit., p. 6.

Therefore, money is neutral and Say's law surreptitiously casts its dark shadow over the mythical economic topology. For "it is only in a world of uncertainty and disappointment," Paul Davidson points out, "that money comes into its own as a necessary mechanism for deferring decisions; money has its niche only when we feel queasy about undertaking any actions which will commit our claims on resources onto a path which can only be altered, if future events require this, at very high costs (if at all)."[7]

Joan Robinson herself has, however, been aware of this shortcoming. She has always cautioned that "Golden Age" economies are simply myths. In 1977 she wrote: "The monetary characteristics of a growing economy would generate instability even if the 'real forces' developed smoothly."[8] Nevertheless, the inadvertent subjugation of monetary institutions to real factors by the pioneers of post-Keynesian theory obscured the desirability of investigating some of the undesirable operations of existing financial institutions. This important gap is now in the process of being filled by Hyman P. Minsky, Paul Davidson, Robert Clower, Axel Leijonhufvud, and others.

Turning now to the gap in microeconomics, it will be recalled that the Anglo-Italian School members had a strong aversion towards general equilibrium analysis. This was probably an overkill reaction on their part. For general equilibrium has advanced far beyond Walras' original framework. "Moreover," Michio Morishima observes, "general equilibrium analysis is not identical with marginal analysis economics. Even though we agreed to reject all the marginal analysis from economics, general equilibrium would still remain as an important, indispensable technique of economic analysis."[10] As we know, even the

---

[7]Paul Davidson, Money and the Real World.

[8]Joan Robinson, "What Are The Questions?," Journal of Economic Literature, Vol. 4, No. 4, December 1977, p. 1321.

[9]See Paul Davidson, op. cit.; Hyman P. Minsky, John Maynard Keynes, op. cit.; Robert W. Clower, "The Keynesian Counter-Revolution: A Theoretical Appraisal," op. cit., Axel Leijonhufvud, On Keynesian Economics and the Economics of Keynes, op. cit.; and Robert W. Clower and Axel Leijonhufvud, "The Coordination of Economic Activities: A Keynesian Perspective," Papers and Proceedings of the 87th Annual Meeting of the American Economic Association, pp. 182-188.

[10]Michio Morishima, "Pasinetti's Growth and Distribution Revisited," Journal of Economic Literature, Vol. 4, No. 1, March 1977, p. 59.

precursors of the Anglo-Italian School, John von Neumann and Piero Sraffa, employed general equilibrium analysis without simultaneously using marginal concepts. Morishima further points out: "It is true that in the actual world economic variables are often determined not in a simultaneous way but in a causal way, but we are not provided with economics minute by minute, but only month by month, quarter by quarter or, in many cases, year by year. . . . In this way we are forced to neglect short lags and regard some group of variables as if they were determined simultaneously."[11] The writers of the Anglo-Italian School generally ignored the empirical side of the problem. Hence, they received Mark Blaug's stricture: "Theory without measurement."[12]

Both Robinson and Kaldor embraced Kalecki's non-competitive mark-up process of the representative firm and then generalized this process to the whole economy as an explanation of price formation. "In terms of strengthening the theory," concedes J.A. Kregel, "it is necessary to find out just how prices are formed and how they function in a capitalistic system. This leads directly to re-thinking of the concepts of markets and purchases and sales relations."[13] This important gap is now in the process of being filled by the recent developments of disequilibrium analysis with its blending of elements from organization theory, information theory, "false trading," reservation price, quantity adjustments and so on under conditions of risk and uncertainty. Clower, Leijonhufvud, Kornai, and others are the current architects of this theory.[14] There is no doubt that some sort of reconstituted general equilibrium theory will serve as the microfoundation for macroeconomics.

---

[11] Michio Morishima, op. cit., p. 59.

[12] Mark Blaug, The Cambridge Revolution: Success or Failure, revised edition, Hobert Paperback No. 6 (London: The Institute of Economic Affairs, 1975), p. 81.

[13] J.A. Kregel, The Reconstruction of Political Economy, op. cit., pp. 207-208.

[14] For example, see J. Kornai, Anti-Equilibrium: On Economic Systems Theory and The Task of Research (Amsterdam: North-Holland, 1971) and Edmund S. Phelp et al., Microeconomic Foundations of Employment and Inflation Theory (New York: W.W. Norton, 1970).

We are living in another exciting epoch of great
transformations in economics. New ideas are percolating
all around and a new synthesis is in the offing. History
of economic thought has shown us that mainstream economics
has been very resilient. It has survived the attacks
from both the left and the right. In undergoing each se-
vere survival test, it has learned valuable lessons from
the Romanticists, the Historical School, the Socialists,
and the Institutionalists. Since the post-Keynesian
writers are not advocating a fundamental change in institutions,[15] mainstream economics will most likely survive
this new test. In the words of Mark Blaug:

> Anyone who has been attentive to the recent
> resurgence of the neoclassical research pro-
> gramme in regional analysis, urban economics,
> applied welfare economics, cost-benefit anal-
> ysis, the economics of education, labour econ-
> omics, the economics of crime, the economics
> of fertility, the economics of marriage, the
> economics of private property rights - the
> list is really endless -- can hardly doubt
> that there is life yet in the concepts of
> maximisation, equilibrium, substitution,
> and all the other tricks of the trade of
> mainstream economics.[16]

References

Baumol, W.J., Economic Theory and Operations Analysis
(Englewood Cliffs, N.J.: Prentice-Hall, 1977).

Blaug, M., The Cambridge Revolution: Success or Failure
(London: The Institute of Economic Affairs, 1975).

Clower, R.W., and Leijonhufvud, A., "The Coordination of
Economic Activities: A Keynesian Perspective,"
Papers and Proceedings of the 87th Annual Meeting of
the American Economic Association, pp. 182-188.

---

[15]See Alfred S. Eichner, op. cit., and Alfred S. Eichner
and J.A. Kregel, "An Essay on Post-Keynesian Theory: A
New Paradigm in Economics," op. cit.

[16]Mark Blaug, op. cit., pp. 85-86.

Davidson, P., Money and the Real World

Eichner, A.S., "Post-Keynesian Theory: An Introduction,"
    Challenge, Vol. 21, No. 2, May/June 1978.

_____, and Kregel, J.A., "An Essay on Post-Keynes-
    ian Theory: A New Paradigm in Economics," Journal
    of Economic Literature, Vol. XIII, December 1975.

Keynes, J.M., The General Theory of Employment Interest
    and Money (London: Macmillan, 1951).

Kornai, J., Anti-Equilibrium: On Economic Systems Theory
    and the Task of Research (Amsterdam: North-Holland,
    1971).

Kregel, J.A., Rate of Profit, Distribution and Growth:
    Two Views (London: Macmillan, 1971).

_____, The Reconstruction of Political Economy:
    An Introduction to Post-Keynesian Economics (New York: John
    Wiley & Sons, 1973).

Leijonhufvud, A., On Keynesian Economics and the Econ-
    omics of Keynes (New York: Oxford University Press,
    1968).

Minsky, H.P., John Maynard Keynes

Morishima, M., "Pasinetti's Growth and Distribution Re-
    visited," Journal of Economic Literature, Vol. 4,
    March 1977.

Phelp, E.S., Microeconomic Foundation of Employment and
    Inflation Theory (New York: W.W. Norton, 1970).

Robinson, J., "What Are The Questions?," Journal of
    Economic Literature, Vol. 4, December 1977.

INDEX

acceleration principle of investment, 11, 12, 158

alternative paradigm (post-Keynesian growth theory), 4, 5, 8, 16, 17, 144

Anglo-Italian school (post-Keynesian, neo-Ricardians), 3n, 17, 114, 126, 136, 153, 173

Asimakopoulos, A., 116n, 117

Austrian theory of capital, see Bohm-Bawerk

Baumol, William J., 100n, 173

Blaug, Mark, 12n, 13n, 15n, 23, 25n, 28n, 127n, 176, 177

Bohm-Bawerk: Austrian theory of capital, 28, 127, 131

canonical equations, 101

capital: accumulation, 36, 58, 59, 64, 66, 89, 98; and the rate of profit, 14], 145, 146, 163; capital deepening, 31, 32; heterogeneous, 49, 51; capital-labor ratio, 29, 31, 36, 60, 69, 74, 76, 77, 86, 89; capital-labor substitution, 15, 16, 49, 50, 165; capital-output ratio, 11, 12; real homogeneous, 4, 27, 28, 50, 52, 141; reversal and double switching, 5, 8, 125,]26, 131-38, 150; capital widening, 31, 32, 99

capitalist system, 14, 18, 93, 113, 114

Champernowne, D.G., 118n, 121n, 126

Clark, John Bates, 28, 52

Clower, R.W., 2, 3n, 4n, 176

Cobb-Douglas production function, 44, 45, 49

comparative dynamics, 65, 66, 67

Darwinian evolutionary theory, 114

distribution and growth, 8, 111, 148, 149, 154, 158, 169

Domar, 10n, 16, 18; Domar's model, 7; knife-edge, 19

Dorfman, Robert; 94

equilibrium: dynamic, 98, uniqueness and stability of, 70, 81; full-employment, 11; static general, causal determinacy and uniqueness of, 74, 74

Eichner, Alfred S., 3n, 5, 144n, 145n, 173, 174, 177n

factor price frontier 31

Ferguson, C.E., 2n, 4n, 14n, 15n, 26, 27n, 28n, 125, 150, 151, 157n

Fisher, F.M., 49n

golden age growth, 15, 35, 37, 43, 46, 56, 117, 148, 161, 174; golden age line, 38; golden age path, 82, 87, 88, 117, 147, 161, 162, 168, 169, 170; golden rule, 89; golden rule of accumulation, 8, 104

growth: full-employment equilibrium, 6, 15, 153, 155; natural rate of (Harrod's), 14, 15, 117, 158, 159; steady state, 18, 55, 60, 61, 65, 66, 72, 86, 90, 166; warranted rate of (Harrod's), 11, 12, 14, 15, 19, 159

Hamiltonian, 100

Harcourt, G.C., 3n, 5, 15n, 29, 130, 134, 136n

Harrod, R.F., 14, 16, 43n, 111, 112, 117; Harrodian knife-edge problem, 6, 14, 15, 16, 17, 35 35; model, 7, 11, 35, 118

Hicks, J.R., 1, 17, 45n, 94n; Hicksian revolution, 26n; trade cycles, 17

historical time, 6, 40, 116, 142

Inada derivative conditions (boundary conditions), 2, 39, 82

interest rate, 43, 50, 57, 65, 67, 125, 127, 132; compound interest effect, 133

179

putty-putty vintage model, 49, 50

real balances, 56, 57, 58, 59, 63, 67

real wage, 30, 48, 75, 111, 130

real rental on capital, 75, 111, 130

reswitching debate, see capital reversal and double switching

Ricardo, David, 23, 111, 112, 113 112, 126, 132, 142, 158; Ricardian economics: value theory, 24; differential rent, 50

Robinson, Joan, 5n, 6, 40, 53, 93n, 113n, 115, 116, 118, 126, 130, 131n, 135n, 136, 141, 142n, 143n, 145n, 146n, 147n, 148n, 149n, 150n

Ruth Cohen's curiosum, 135

Rybczynski: line, 86, 87, 89; theorem, 83, 84, 85

Samuelson, P.A., 1, 2, 3, 35, 133, 136, 137

saving, 11, 12, 17, 35, 40, 55, 58, 59, 66, 67, 74, 77, 79, 90, 126, 149

Say's law, 35, 175

socialist economy, 93

Solow, R.M., 1, 9n, 15, 16n, 32, 35, 45n, 49n, 50, 73n, 125, 164

Sraffa, P., 111n, 126, 131, 132, 133, 141, 176

technical progress, 149, 165, 168, Harrod-neutral (disembodied), 44, 45, 46, 47, 50; Hicks neutral, 45; labor-augmenting, 14, 15, 43, 45, 47; capital-augmenting, 45; Solow-neutral, 45

trade cycles (Hicks), 17

transversality condition, 98

uncertainty, 6, 55, 146

Uzawa, H., 8

control variable, 103

costate variable, 100

vintage machines, 49, 50, 167

von Neumann, John, 111, 118, 121, 176

wage-rental ratio, 81, 86, 89

Walrasian general equilibrium analysis, 26

welfare economics, 94

Wicksell, Knut, 126, 127-130; neutral price Wicksell effect, 134; price Wicksell effect, 131

widow's cruse theory of distribution, 7, 17, 112, 115, 126, 155, 167